SECRETS OF CHAKRAS

SECRETS OF
CHAKRAS

JENNIE HARDING

IVY PRESS

First published in the UK in 2018 by
Ivy Press
An imprint of The Quarto Group
The Old Brewery, 6 Blundell Street
London N7 9BH, United Kingdom
T (0)20 7700 6700 **F** (0)20 7700 8066
www.QuartoKnows.com

British Library Cataloguing-in-Publication Data
A catalogue record for this book is available from the British Library

ISBN: 978-1-78240-571-9

This book was conceived, designed and produced by
Ivy Press
58 West Street, Brighton BN1 2RA, United Kingdom

Publisher: Susan Kelly
Creative Director: Michael Whitehead
Editorial Director: Tom Kitch
Art Director: James Lawrence
Designer: Ginny Zeal
Illustrator: Nicky Ackland-Snow
Photographer: Neal Grundy
Models: Nicola Jane Hobbs and Joe Menzies
Hair and Make-up: Justine Rice
Editorial Assistant: Niamh Jones

Printed in China

10 9 8 7 6 5 4 3 2 1

Note from the publisher
Information given in this book is not intended to be taken as a
replacement for medical advice. Any person with a condition
requiring medical attention should consult a qualified medical
practitioner or therapist.

Cover image: Shutterstock/ViSnezh

HOW TO USE THIS BOOK

Welcome to the world of the chakras: you are about to begin a fascinating journey into the energy centres within the human body. This book is a manual to help you learn more about the chakras, what they are, where they are located and how they affect you physically, mentally and spiritually. By reading it, you will gain a new understanding of what it is to be and live in a human body. This book is divided into sections to make learning about the chakras easy and fun. To get started, it's a good idea to read the book through as a whole; you may then find sections you are drawn to revisit because they are more relevant to you. Exploring the chakras can be a very inspiring and individual experience.

Important notice

Simple yoga postures are shown in this book as a method to energize the chakras. If you are pregnant or have any medical condition, you should consult a doctor before attempting yoga practice. Also, the information in this book is not intended to replace medical advice; if you feel you have any physical or psychological conditions, you should always consult a doctor.

Background

We start by exploring the nature of the chakras, their ancient meaning and their links to the practice of yoga.

The Sacral Chakra: Introduction & Colour

The Sacral Chakra is the second energy level in the chakra system. It is the place of emotions, linked to the relationships happening in your life. All of our interactions with family, friends, partners, spouses or children have the potential to either nourish or deplete this chakra, even if you live alone, you can still experience it in relationship to yourself. Sacral Chakra energy is fundamental to human life. A simple affirmation for the Sacral Chakra is, 'I feel,' showing this is a place of great sensitivity.

The colour of the sacral chakra is a warm orange. This is a bright, positive and attractive colour, with a radiance that encourages self-confidence and openness. There is a sunny and cheerful feel to this shade, a sense of expansion and freedom, like the joy of summer and being outdoors or the excitement of holidays in bright locations.

Generative power
The Sacral Chakra is also the sexual centre, its energy speeds into all the organs and systems associated with reproduction. Keeping the Sacral Chakra well-energized and healthy is particularly important if you are intending to start a family, and that applies to both partners in the relationship. In the East, the energetic health of potential parents is considered to be as important as their physical health, so chakra balancing is a good thing to work on to ensure conception happens in the best physical and energetic framework.

Working with the Sacral Chakra also helps to keep all emotional and sexual relationships balanced and healthy.

Receiving satisfaction
Another aspect of the Sacral Chakra is abundance. Sometimes the idea of abundance gets mixed up with prosperity, it can mean money, but it also means receiving positive energy in all aspects of your life. When the Sacral Chakra is low in energy, this cuts off the flow of abundance and it shows up as feelings of lack or worries like, 'There isn't enough.' Restoring warm Sacral energy is a truly positive way to get abundant energy flowing again.

Discovering the chakras

Each chakra is looked at individually, giving you simple suggestions for ways to experience its effect and how to re-energize it.

The new chakras

The third chapter introduces five additional spiritual levels that have been added to the basic seven chakras.

The Alta Major or Occipital Chakra

The Alta Major Chakra sits at the back of the cranium, right under the skull where the head and neck meet. If you feel the spot with your fingers, there is a slight indentation there, you can feel it when you move your head up and down. The Alta Major Chakra is connected to the occipital area at the back of the brain. It links to the Throat and Third Eye Chakras, once again as a means of higher energy expression. Sometimes the Alta Major Chakra is referred to as a place of dreaming, where visions and intuitive information from the Third Eye Chakra can be expanded, and then communicated via the Throat Chakra. This is a chakra with a deeply psychic effect, best explored with a teacher as a guide.

The colour of the Alta Major Chakra is usually considered to be magenta, a deep reddish-purple colour. It is an expression of the deep red of the Root Chakra travelling up the spine and combining with the purple of the Crown Chakra: a meeting between earth and heaven.

Rainbow moonstone
The Alta Major Chakra can be energized by wearing rainbow moonstone. This beautiful iridescent crystal shines in mystical rainbow colours depending on the light, it can also be placed into a crystal healing matrix for the same purpose.

Jasmine essential oil
In aromatherapy, the rich, warm and heady aroma of jasmine absolute is a beautiful support to the Alta Major Chakra. It is expensive, but can be sourced already diluted in jojoba oil ready to apply to the skin. A few drops of jasmine in jojoba placed on the location of the Alta Major Chakra at the back of the head can be deeply soothing and supportive.

Chakra healing

A variety of different healing methods are introduced to allow you to work with chakra energy.

Crystals & Chakra Healing

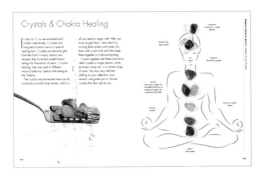

In Section 2, as we explored each chakra individually, a crystal was designed to each one as a special healing tool. Crystals are beautiful gifts from the Earth in many colours and shapes, they have fascinated human beings for thousands of years. In crystal healing, they are used in different ways to balance, restore and energize the chakras.

The crystals recommended here are all available as small tumble stones, which is all you need to begin with. After you have bought them, clean them by running them under cold water, dry them with a soft cloth and then keep them together in a drawstring bag. Crystal suppliers sell these and many other crystals in larger pieces, some polished, some raw, or a whole range of sizes. You may very well start adding to your collection, your intuition will guide you to choose crystals that feel right to you.

Chakras for life

The final chapters take you into your everyday life, showing you how to use chakra awareness to be more invigorated and empowered at work, in your relationships and at home.

Root Chakra: Home as a Sanctuary Space

The idea of home as a safe place is deeply rooted in human consciousness.

In the 1950s, a psychologist called Abraham Maslow created a model called the hierarchy of needs.

In some ways this diagram resembles our chakra chart: at the bottom are two levels linked to basic needs, then the middle levels are psychological needs, and the upper level is linked to self-fulfilment.

At the level of basic needs, security and safety, along with physical survival needs like food and shelter, are vital to human mental and physical well-being. If there is a deep sense of grounding and rooting and feeling secure in that place.

Your own place
How do you feel in your home? Does it feel like a safe place to come back to? This doesn't necessarily mean having bolts on the doors and windows and a security alarm here, it's more about how your home is working as a sanctuary for you. This is linked to Root Chakra energy. Do you feel you belong, in your home? How does the energy of your home sort out, inside and out? If you have chosen your home yourself, most likely it will suit you, however, if you have had to move somewhere that is not entirely your choice, you may feel less at ease.

Emotional home-making
Using an express ceremony is a wonderful way to clear the space inside your home before adding some Root Chakra energy. Use a stick of your favourite incense or some sage leaves burned in a charcoal brazier in a small fireproof dish. As the smoke burns, proclaim your Root Chakra meditation to feel new, present and grounded in your space. Plant a pretty crystal or two in a central function in your space to protect you from any negative energies in your environment. By placing Root Chakra energy into your space to build yourself a personal sanctuary.

DISCOVERING THE CHAKRAS

In this section we will explore the chakras themselves, in order to find out what they actually are and where the idea of them originally came from. The chakras are part of an ancient energy system which helps to balance body, mind and spirit. Be ready for some visualizations and other exercises to try – the best way to learn about the chakras is to begin experiencing the way they feel to you.

What Are the Chakras?

The chakras are a way of representing life energy, the vital force that inhabits and energizes the body. They form a circuit in which this energy flows through each centre and onto the next, and as it flows, it nourishes and supports the physical body.

The map of the chakras shows seven major centres along the spine. These are represented as colours of the rainbow: red at the base of the spine, orange in the lower abdomen, yellow in the gap between the ribs, green in the middle of the chest, pale blue at the throat, dark blue between the eyebrows and purple at the top of the head.

The chakras also have significant names. 'Root' indicates that this centre is stabilizing. 'Sacral' refers to the triangular bone at the base of the spine, called the sacrum. 'Solar plexus' relates to the nerve centre or 'plexus' in the stomach area, the place where you feel 'butterflies in the stomach' when you are stressed. 'Heart' refers not to the physical heart itself, but to the central point of balance of the whole system: you can see three chakras above and three below it. The 'Throat' chakra is found in the centre of the throat area. The 'Third Eye' is a location between the eyebrows linked to the pineal gland in the brain. The 'Crown' is the top of the head where you would wear a crown; pictures of saints with halos around their heads also symbolize this area.

'Chakra' is a Sanskrit word from India; it means wheel. These centres are not static as they look on this diagram; they spin, and they also go through the body from front to back. The physical spine is the connection between them; life energy, called 'prana' in Sanskrit, flows along the spine and through the chakras in a constant loop.

On pages 14–15 you will discover how to use your breathing to feel energy coming into your body and passing through the chakra centres.

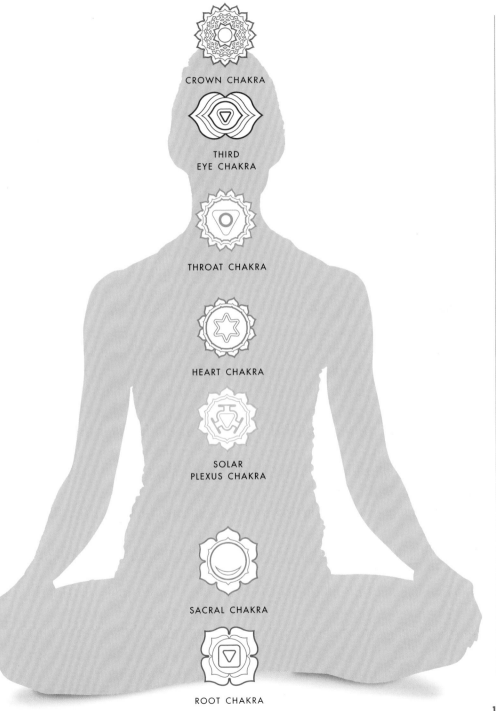

CROWN CHAKRA

THIRD
EYE CHAKRA

THROAT CHAKRA

HEART CHAKRA

SOLAR
PLEXUS CHAKRA

SACRAL CHAKRA

ROOT CHAKRA

Origins of the Chakras

Bringing East to West

Swami Vivekenanda was one of many inspired Indian teachers who originally brought yoga and its philosophy to the Western world.

Yoga and the West

In the 1890s, spiritual teachers from India such as Swami Vivekananda (1863–1902) toured the USA and Europe to encourage links between East and West. Notable teachers of yoga such as Swami Sivananda (1887–1963), B.K.S. Iyengar (1918–2014) and Krishnamacharya (1888–1989) encouraged the spread of different styles of yoga and the philosophies associated with it right across the Western world. In the 1950s, Americans Theos Bernard and Richard Hittleman travelled to India study yoga and its principles, and then returned to teach it themselves. The 1960s saw an explosion of interest in yoga and the culture and philosophies of India, with figures such as the Maharishi Mahesh Yogi teaching meditation to Westerners. Currently, yoga and meditation are two of the most popular stress-relieving practices all over the world.

The chakra system is a fundamental aspect of yoga, which is a Sanskrit word meaning 'union'; it is a practice of seeking the unity of body, mind and spirit through adopting different healing postures called 'asanas'. Yoga evolved from a very ancient Indian system of medicine, healing, spirituality and holistic living called Ayurveda, another Sanskrit word meaning 'knowledge of life'. Ayurveda is thousands of years old, and Ayurvedic medicine is still practised in India and all around the world today. Yoga, and the revitalizing and re-energizing system of the chakras, are a branch of this ancient healing system.

Today, the chakra system derived from yoga is also used to underpin holistic healing. The life energy circuit of the chakras is linked to many healing therapies such as Reiki, reflexology, crystal healing, colour healing, spiritual healing and aromatherapy.

Keeping notes
You may wish to keep a record of this visualization to help your practice.

FEELING ENERGY THROUGH THE CHAKRAS As well as learning about chakras in theory, it is important to start experiencing them for yourself. Here is a simple exercise to start feeling energy coming in and out of your body, flowing through all the chakra centres.

1 *Sit comfortably on a chair with a firm back so you are balanced and supported. Your feet need to be uncrossed and placed flat on the floor, your back straight and your hands resting lightly in your lap. Take a few deep breaths and relax.*

2 *Breathe lightly and calmly throughout this exercise. Close your eyes.*

3 *Feel your feet in contact with the floor. Imagine golden energy rising up into your feet from deep within the earth, flowing up your legs and into the base of your spine.*

4 *Next, imagine the energy travelling up through your abdomen to your ribs. As you breathe in deeply, feel it flowing into the centre of your chest.*

5 *Then picture it rising up through your throat to the place between your eyebrows. Feel it there for a moment or two, and then feel it flowing up to the crown of your head. Imagine the energy passing out of the top of your head, connecting you to the stars.*

6 *Now, as you take a new breath, imagine white light coming in through the top of your head, like a fountain, flowing through the place between your eyebrows, down through your throat, through your chest and abdomen, down to the base of your spine, on through your legs and out through your feet, into the earth. That completes one circuit of the life energy called prana, flowing through all your chakras. You can build this 'energy loop' by continuing to breathe in through your feet to your crown, then breathing out from your crown down to your feet.*

7 *To finish, breathe deeply a few times, then open your eyes. Notice how you feel within yourself.*

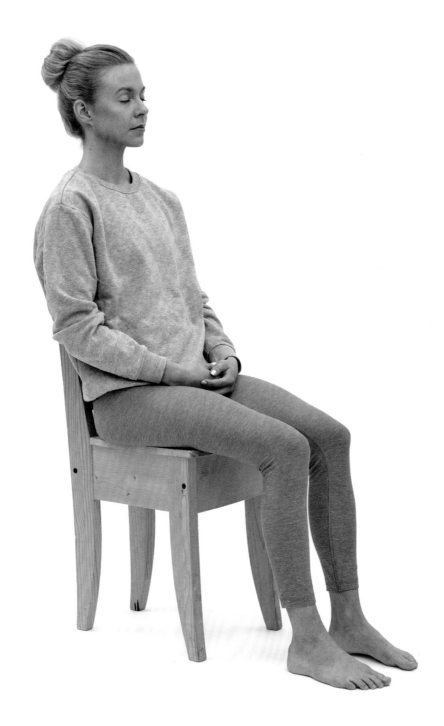

Sanskrit Names of the Chakras

We have already seen that the seven major chakras along the spine are usually given their Western names: Root, Sacral, Solar Plexus, Heart, Throat, Third Eye and Crown. In India, each chakra has an ancient and special name, and understanding these helps to deepen our understanding of these centres.

From this chart you can see that the meanings of the Sanskrit names hold new clues about the energies of the chakras. Linking Muladhara, 'root support' to Sahasrara, the 'thousand-petalled lotus', shows that in order to find enlightenment, it is also important to be 'rooted' to earth. Svadhisthana, 'one's own abode', is often an area (the sacrum) where emotional stress can cause aches and pains. Manipura, 'jewel place', is how the solar plexus area should feel, and again it is a common place where tension is felt instead. Anahata, the heart, is called 'unhurt', yet feelings in the heart can cause such turmoil. Vishuddha, 'especially pure', is in the throat from which we speak – and not always kindly. Ajna, 'command', is the third eye in the forehead, where mental stress can cause headaches.

Western Chakra Name	Sanskrit Chakra Name
Root	Muladhara
Sacral	Svadhisthana
Solar Plexus	Manipura
Heart	Anahata
Throat	Vishuddha
Third Eye	Ajna
Crown	Sahasrara

Understanding these ancient names adds another layer of meaning to the chakras, showing the potential for their effects on body and mind.

Meaning	Symbol

'Root support', linking to the grounding effect of this chakra.
Its element is earth.

From two Sanskrit words 'swa' – 'one's own'; and
'adhisthana' – 'abode' or 'seat'. Its element is water.

From two Sanskrit words: 'mani' – jewel; and 'pura' – place.
Its element is fire.

In Sanskrit, 'Anahata' means 'unhurt'.
Its element is air.

'Vishuddha' means 'especially pure'.
Its element is ether.

'Ajna' means 'command'. It is the first of the two
most spiritual chakras, beyond the elements.

In Sanskrit, 'Sahasrara' means 'thousand-petalled';
this refers to the image of the thousand-petalled lotus,
the symbol of enlightenment.

How the Chakras Interact with the Body

The flow of energy
Ancient Eastern healing systems like acupuncture maintain that the human body also has an energy system that influences all aspects of life.

By now you may be wondering, 'So how do the chakras work with the physical body?' The first thing to remember is that these are energy centres, not anatomical structures. In the West this concept is sometimes unfamiliar; mainstream Western medicine and science reject the idea of an energy system within the body. In the East, however, healing systems like Ayurveda in India, acupuncture in China or shiatsu in Japan are centuries old, and all are based on the idea of energy permeating the physical body, flowing within it and influencing it throughout life.

In the early twentieth century, famous Western esoteric teachers such as Alice Bailey began to link the chakras with the hormone glands of the body. This connection continues to underpin current holistic healing practice. The endocrine system is a delicate aspect of human physiology where the brain communicates with the body and influences its function.

For example, the adrenal glands, situated above your kidneys, produce a number of hormones like adrenaline and cortisol; mental and emotional stress affect the brain, and this stimulates the glands, which may begin to over-produce hormones, and so create imbalance. The adrenal glands are linked to the Sacral Chakra, so working to balance that chakra can help that brain-body link and improve wellbeing.

It is still important to remember that chakras affect the body in very subtle ways; using the hormone system is a Western way of explaining the Eastern concept of life energy.

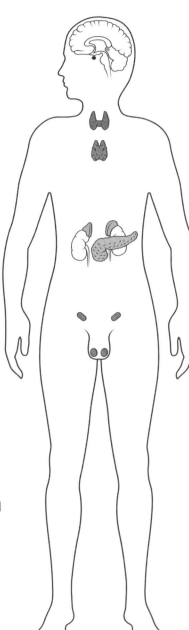

 Third eye Chakra

Gland: Pituitary gland
Hormone function:
The master hormone gland, influencing the whole body

 Throat Chakra

Gland: Thyroid gland
Hormone function:
Regulates body metabolism and temperature

 Sacral Chakra

Gland: Adrenal glands
Hormone function:
The centre for stress hormone balance

 Root Chakra

Gland: Reproductive glands (testes in men, ovaries in women)
Hormone function: Reproductive functions

 Crown Chakra

Gland: Pineal gland
Hormone function:
Regulates sleep and other biological cycles

 Heart Chakra

Gland: Thymus gland in the middle of the chest
Hormone function:
Part of the immune system

 Solar Plexus Chakra

Gland: Pancreas
Hormone function:
Influences metabolism and blood–sugar balance

THE CHAKRAS & YOGA

Chakras underpin the practice of yoga. The postures or asanas of yoga work to bend and flex the spine, which is the main physical channel along which the chakras sit. Different yoga postures work on specific chakras; visualizing the chakra opening and energy flowing through it during the posture is a very effective way of re-energizing it.

In a typical yoga class, many different postures will be worked through in sequence, so that by the end of the session the whole system should feel much more balanced. Here are some examples of yoga postures linked to different chakras.

For now, these poses are just for illustration. In chapter 2, we will be exploring each of the chakras in detail; each one will have a detailed yoga posture to go with it with full instructions on how to enter, stay in and leave the pose.

Apanasana: the Knee to Chest Pose
Lying on the back with the legs out straight, one knee is pulled up against the chest. This allows the Root Chakra to be pressed deep into the ground.

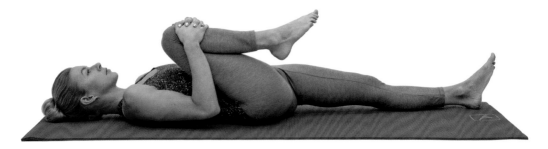

Halasana: the Plough

Lying down, the legs come up and over the back of the head, with the feet resting on the floor (this is a pose that is more challenging and is best shown by a teacher). In the pose, the Throat Chakra is stimulated.

Bhujangasana: the Cobra

From lying face down, the arms support the chest and help to lift the torso off the ground. This opens the chest and stimulates the Heart Chakra.

Balasana: the Child's Pose

Crouching down and tucking in all the limbs into a 'womb-like' posture relaxes the entire body and is also very good for resting and rebalancing the Sacral Chakra.

THE CHAKRAS & HOLISTIC THERAPIES

The chakra system with its seven rainbow colours – red, orange, yellow, green, pale blue, dark blue and violet – has become a vital element in many holistic healing therapies. Here are some methods linked to the chakra system.

Colour healing

This type of healing is given by someone who channels the colours of the chakras through their hands directly onto the body. The person receiving the healing simply lies in a relaxed position. The person giving the healing is the one who can see the colours; the person receiving may feel the effect as 'warmer' when the red, orange or yellow rays are being channelled, or 'cooler' when the green, blue and purple rays are being used. Colour healing does not necessarily concentrate on the chakra locations on the back; it can be applied to any part of the body.

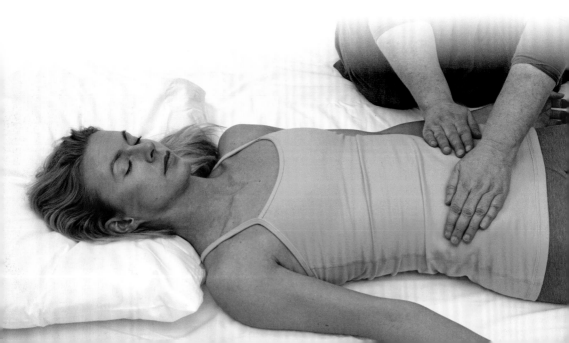

Sound healing with Tibetan bowls

The chakras also respond to different sounds. For centuries in Tibet, special bowls handmade with unique combinations of metals have been tuned to musical notes which benefit different chakras. The bowls are 'played' by running a carved wooden stick around the rim; this releases the note in the bowl. As the bowl releases its note and vibrates, it can be placed next to the person receiving the healing, or even on part of the body. The sounds released by the bowls are extremely soothing and beneficial to the brain.

Crystal healing

Crystals and stones can be found in many different colours and shades; these correspond with the colours of the chakras. Crystal healing involves placing stones on different parts of the body to rebalance chakras and restore the body. The crystal healer chooses the stones they feel will enhance the energy of the person they are treating and places them where they will bring most benefit.

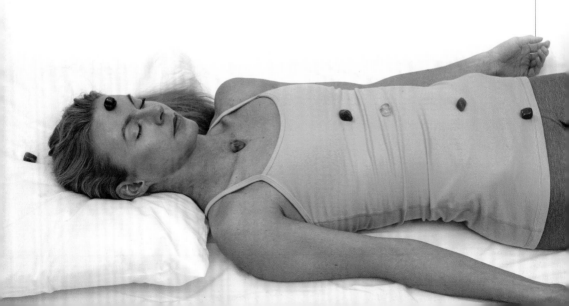

Picking Up Signs of Chakra Energy

O ver the next few pages we are going to look at how to sense the energies of your chakras. You may be surprised at how your feelings, experiences or ways you interact with other people may show particular chakra energies are low or out of balance. Once you understand the signs, you can begin to work with chakra energy to restore inner balance, with potential physical, emotional and mental benefits.

You may be wondering, 'How is it that different experiences I'm having link to chakra energy?' Remember, the chakra system permeates the physical body and works in tandem with it. Different feelings, emotions and sensations trigger the different chakras to react. Over time, if the same feelings and emotions keep on happening, then a particular chakra will interact with the body and give you signals. The chakras help your body to communicate with you.

Root Chakra signs

If you are feeling vulnerable or unsupported in your life, or if you are anxious about material or physical survival, then it is likely that your Root Chakra needs restoring. This is the base of the chakra system; when you look at a typical diagram of all the chakras, the shape of the person sitting is a triangle, and the foundation of the triangle is what makes it solid and stable. The Root Chakra sits at the base of the spine to provide strong positive energy to the whole system. If you are feeling lower backaches or deep physical tiredness, these are also signs of low Root Chakra energy. Working to restore and re-energize the Root Chakra helps to give you renewed confidence and strength. On pages 34–43 you will find methods to help revive the Root Chakra.

Sacral Chakra signs

At the front of the body the Sacral Chakra sits just below the navel, and at the back of the body it relates to the triangular sacrum bone in the lower back. Sacral Chakra energy is linked to the emotions, to intimate relationships or more generally to how you feel in your interactions with others. If you lack self-confidence or you feel that in your relationships, people tend to override your feelings, then it is likely your Sacral Chakra needs energizing. This chakra also influences the genito-urinary systems of the body, so signs like persistent urinary infections can be associated with it. Replenishing Sacral energy brings renewed feelings of confidence and vitality. On pages 46–55 you will find ways to restore the Sacral Chakra.

Solar Plexus Chakra signs

The Solar Plexus Chakra sits at the top of the abdomen, just under the curve of the ribs. It is one of the most common places to feel mental and emotional stress. Exam nerves, performance anxiety, going for an interview, visiting the dentist; any time you have to face something that scares you and feel tightness or 'butterflies' in the stomach, this is the effect of triggering the Solar Plexus Chakra. Repeated situations that cause stress can deplete this chakra very quickly. On pages 58–67 you will find ways to replenish and restore this chakra, bringing feelings of confidence and self-belief.

Heart Chakra signs

As we saw earlier in the book, the Heart Chakra should not be confused with the physical organ of the heart. It is, instead, the point of balance of the seven chakra centres at the centre of the whole system. Three chakras sit below it and three above it. The Heart Chakra is linked to love, compassion, peace and harmony. It is deeply affected by emotional upsets or heartbreak, which can sometimes be felt as physical pain as well. The break-up of relationships, loss of a partner or bereavement are all deep triggers for the Heart Chakra, which is a highly sensitive energy centre. On pages 70–79 you will find ways to support and heal this chakra so love can be a source of renewal in your life.

Throat Chakra signs

Located at the base of your neck, this is the place of the voice, for speaking and singing, for expression, for telling your story to the world. Feeling unable to speak because of emotional or social pressures will affect this chakra; persistent sore throats or feelings of restriction in the throat show that it needs help. Restoring this chakra gives you faith in yourself, in the truth of who you are, and encourages you to express yourself with your own voice. On pages 82–91 you will find ways to restore and re-energize the Throat Chakra.

Third Eye Chakra signs

The Third Eye Chakra sits just above the gap between the eyebrows. It is an energy centre that expands inner vision and intuition, especially through meditation practice. Feelings of resistance to new ideas or unwillingness to learn new things can be signs of a lack of confidence in the Third Eye Chakra; stress headaches across the forehead and mental tension are also signs that this chakra needs help. When it is restored, the mind is open to intuitive guidance and ready to experience creative thinking. On pages 94–103 you will find methods to help balance and restore the Third Eye Chakra.

Crown Chakra signs

The Crown Chakra is the highest chakra with the connection to Source, spirit, God, however you perceive spiritual energy. It is a deeply subtle chakra, best activated consciously when all the other chakras have been cleared and restored. Persistent headaches or disturbed dreams can be signs of imbalance. On pages 106–115 you will find ways to balance and replenish the Crown Chakra.

The Chakras:
A Path of Exploration

Feel your own inspiration
Starting your personal journey into the chakras is exciting – it is a way to learn more about yourself and apply your insights to your life.

Working with the chakras is a fascinating path into the different energy levels. By understanding them more deeply you can work with the seven chakras and feel their benefits in your daily life.

A pilgrimage into the chakras is like following an 'energy map': each chakra is an important signpost showing you different kinds of information. Some aspects you can understand with your mind or see with your eyes; others you need to experience in your body or by developing your awareness of your own inner world. To test this out, you will need to stop, pause, breathe and sense. This is important: energy work is about experiencing different states of being, and of course, most of the time we are all far too busy doing.

Going through the rest of this book, you will find many different ways to work with your chakras and feel their effects. Some will feel more relevant to you than others. Always trust your intuition to guide you. This is your personal voyage: follow the suggestions that feel right to you.

It's a good idea to start a notebook (maybe get yourself a set of coloured felt-tip pens) so you can makes notes or doodle or draw things related to your experiences in the colours of the chakras you are working on.

The main thing is: enjoy your journey!

PROFILES OF THE SEVEN CHAKRAS

The seven individual chakras are explored in detail in this chapter. Discover how to locate and be aware of each chakra, and how to know when they need support. Many tools and ideas are suggested to help you feel, experience and re-energize all the chakras. Reading this section is like a journey in itself, taking you through all seven chakra energies, illustrating how rich a path of discovery this can be.

The Root Chakra:
Introduction & Colour

The first chakra in our energy map is the Root Chakra. Root Chakra energy is bright, vibrant, warm and energizing. It gives strength to the body and restores physical wellbeing, channelling the energy of action, practical creativity and regeneration. When the Root Chakra is working, great ideas can become physical reality: what is in the head actually takes shape. For example, you might think endlessly about that holiday you want to take, but it isn't real until you are truly on the journey. Your Root Chakra is where you drew the power to get up and go.

The colour of the Root Chakra is red, the deepest, most vibrant crimson shade you can imagine. Red is the colour of blood, which carries life-giving oxygen to our cells and gives us strength and vitality. Red is a stimulating colour, vibrant and energizing to the mind and spirit. In nature, deep red flowers like roses or peonies immediately attract the eye, opening the rich depths of their colour in an inviting display.

Living securely

Red Root Chakra energy is what keeps us grounded and stable on the earth. A simple affirmation for it is 'I live.' It makes us feel physically strong and secure, both within ourselves and in everyday life. It gives us energy to act, to take positive steps with inner confidence, sensing we are 'going in the right direction'. The Root Chakra draws the nourishing energy of the earth into our whole system, supporting and energizing body, mind and spirit.

The Root Chakra is easily depleted by spending too much time in the head and feeling mentally stressed or overloaded. When restored, it helps you feel strong and centred inside, balanced in the present moment, with the energy to move forwards in life.

SENSING THE ROOT CHAKRA
The location of the Root Chakra is right at the base of the spine. If you sit on a chair and rest your hand on your lower back where your spine meets the chair, this is the spot.

If you can sit on the floor, either cross-legged or in the yoga 'lotus' position with the feet on the thighs (not to be attempted unless you are very supple), you will feel an even stronger connection between the base of your spine and where it meets the ground. Feeling 'grounded' is a very important aspect of the Root Chakra: being connected to the earth and drawing its strength up into the body. In the middle of a busy day, just taking a few minutes to sit like this can bring inner peace and mental clarity. It is the best posture for meditation, because it encourages correct spinal alignment for energy to flow through all the chakras.

A stable base
The location of the Root Chakra is a reminder that it is very important to maintain a connection to the earth.

Many people rush around all day and live completely in their heads, controlled by the spin of their minds. Physical issues like lower backache or stiffness, feeling tired or totally lacking in strength, or feeling demotivated with no enthusiasm for doing anything, are signs that the Root Chakra needs help.

The chakra of connection
The Root Chakra also symbolizes belonging, including where your roots are and how connected you feel to the place where you live. Feelings of disconnection and 'not knowing where you are' can be helped by focusing on the Root Chakra.

Fortunately there are many simple ways to restore and re-energize this chakra, bringing a sense of inner strength and renewed vitality.

YOGA POSTURE FOR THE ROOT CHAKRA

On the previous pages we saw that sitting cross-legged can connect the spine to the earth; however, if you are a beginner or not very supple, that can be uncomfortable. In yoga, the Root Chakra can also be energized by a standing posture called Mountain Pose, which allows you to breathe the energy of the earth up the legs, into the base of the spine and into the body.

1 *It's best to have bare feet for this pose. Stand on a firm floor, carpet or a yoga mat. Breathe regularly as you go into the pose; take a few deep breaths when you are in the pose; breathe regularly again as you come out of it.*

Body & Mind

This pose may look simple but it can be quite difficult to maintain, especially at first. 'Standing with focus' like this is strengthening to body and mind, benefitting the spine and posture. It also makes you very aware of the earth beneath your feet.

2 *Stand with your feet together and arms lightly at your sides; if you find it hard to balance, place your feet about six inches apart.*

3 *Concentrate on your feet; lift your toes, spread them and place them back on the mat. Feel your feet very strongly connected to the earth.*

4 *Lift up through your legs, keeping your knees slightly bent. Feel your hips and buttocks are relaxed and facing forwards.*

5 *Stretch up through your torso, feeling your spine expand.*

6 *Expand your chest a little and feel your collarbone stretch outwards; let your arms rest at your sides, fingers pointing down.*

7 *Elongate through your neck and rest your eyes ahead.*

8 *Now inhale, imagining red energy coming up through the earth into your feet, legs, and up into your Root Chakra at the base of your spine. Take a few deep breaths and feel the energy as it moves through your body. Keep*

breathing deeply and steadily. Hold the pose for about a minute, and then gently bend your knees and step out of it.

ROOT CHAKRA MEDITATION

This is a meditation using a mountain theme to re-energize the Root Chakra. Find a quiet space and sit comfortably on a firm-backed chair, feet uncrossed, hands relaxed in your lap. The following passage will guide you on an imaginary journey into the Root Chakra. If you like, you can record yourself reading it aloud so you can listen to it.

Meditation

Take a few slow deep breaths. Feel your body is comfortable and relaxed on the chair. Let your mind be quiet. Let any distracting thoughts just float gently away.

Close your eyes; be aware of the base of your spine, where you feel the chair underneath you. Breathe comfortably, and relax.

Now imagine that you are walking along a path towards a beautiful mountain. It may be one that you have seen before, or it may be purely imaginary. Really focus on the mountain as it rises before you with its base in the earth and its peak in the sky. Feel its power, its stability, its strength at its base; and the rarer, higher energy at its peak where the air is fine, pure and clear.

As you sit and breathe, now imagine that you are the mountain. Your feet, legs and the end of your spine are the base – strong, stable, connected to earth. Breathe in and draw deep red energy up your feet and legs and into the Root Chakra at the base of your spine. Feel the Root Chakra absorb this energy. As you breathe, allow the chakra to be bathed in this red earth healing. Sit like this for a few moments.

Then take a few deep breaths, open your eyes and come back to the room. You may wish to write some notes about how that exercise worked for you, or try and draw the image that you saw.

"Be still
like a mountain"
LAO TZU

OTHER ROOT CHAKRA ENERGIZING IDEAS As well as

yoga postures and meditation, here are some different ideas to use to energize the Root Chakra. These are particularly helpful for people who are constantly living in their heads and are definitely not grounded. Being grounded, in relation to this chakra, means that you have a firm sense of where you are in your life: not just a sense of place, but also a feeling of belonging, of being rooted, knowing, 'Here I am'. Root Chakra energy can also mean being practical and doing things with a warm and creative intent.

Standing barefoot

A simple exercise is to go outside in bare feet and simply stand on the earth, on a lawn or an outdoor green space. Even if it is chilly outside, just doing this for a minute or so, feeling the actual earth beneath your feet can bring you back to the present moment. This is very helpful during times of mental stress.

Digging the soil

Gardening, digging, working with the earth is very beneficial to Root Chakra energy. The work you do in the soil also generates energy to encourage plants to grow. Having your hands in the earth is a great stress-reliever; research has shown that it brings a sense of deep wellbeing.

Cooking from scratch

Kneading dough to bake bread, baking a cake or making a hearty casserole to heat in the oven: these evoke the energy of creating warming, comforting food, not just for yourself but for others too. This is practical work, but good for the body and good for the mind.

Toasty toes

If cooking and gardening sound too complicated, come back to the colour red, the colour of the Root Chakra. If you have cold feet, try wearing bright red socks: the energizing colour stimulates your mind and body to feel the Root Chakra energy.

ROOT CHAKRA ENERGY TOOLS As well as practical things you can do to energize the Root Chakra, you can also use other materials or symbols from nature to enhance its effect in your life.

Red jasper

Red jasper is an easily obtained stone. It is formed of microscopic grains of quartz mixed with the mineral iron oxide, which gives the stone its strong brick-red colour. It is often sold as a 'tumblestone', a small polished pebble. Jasper energizes and supports the Root Chakra; in ancient times, it was often carried or worn as jewellery as a form of psychic protection. If you have to go into a situation that feels intimidating or meet a person whose energy feels overpowering, try carrying a jasper stone in your pocket or in a bag. Knowing it is there will give you a boost of Root Chakra energy to help you feel more confident.

The aroma of benzoin

Benzoin gum comes from Indonesia; it oozes out of the wood of styrax benzoin trees, goes solid when it dries, and is then collected. When benzoin gum is dissolved in alcohol it becomes a resinoid, a thick liquid considered a type of essential oil; it has a reddish colour. Benzoin has a warm, richly sweet, vanilla-like scent which is deeply soothing and comforting. If you put four drops of benzoin into a fragrance burner, a vaporizer or simply onto a tissue on a windowsill, the wonderful rich aroma will spread into your space. Inhaling the aroma complements the Root Chakra meditation or the practice of the Mountain yoga pose by adding the energy of benzoin to the exercises.

KEY ROOT CHAKRA ENERGY TOOLS

| BENZOIN OIL | RED JASPER | MOUNTAIN THEME |

The Sacral Chakra: Introduction & Colour

The Sacral Chakra is the second energy level in the chakra system. It is the place of emotions, linked to the relationships happening in your life. All of our interactions with family, friends, partners, spouses or children have the potential to either nourish or deplete this chakra; even if you live alone, you can still experience it in relationship to yourself. Sacral Chakra energy is fundamental to human life. A simple affirmation for the Sacral Chakra is 'I feel,' showing this is a place of great sensitivity.

The colour of the Sacral Chakra is a warm orange. This is a bright, positive and attractive colour, with a radiance that encourages self-confidence and openness. There is a sunny and cheerful feel to this shade, a sense of expansion and freedom, like the joy of summer and being outdoors or the excitement of holidays in bright locations.

Generative power

The Sacral Chakra is also the sexual centre; its energy spreads into all the organs and systems associated with reproduction. Keeping the Sacral Chakra well-energized and healthy is particularly important if you are intending to start a family, and that applies to both partners in the relationship. In the East, the energetic health of potential parents is considered to be as important as their physical health, so chakra balancing is a good thing to work on to ensure conception happens in the best physical and energetic framework.

Working with the Sacral Chakra also helps to keep all emotional and sexual relationships balanced and healthy.

Receiving satisfaction

Another aspect of the Sacral Chakra is abundance. Sometimes the idea of abundance gets mixed up with prosperity; it can mean money, but it also means receiving positive energy in all aspects of your life. When the Sacral Chakra is low in energy, this cuts off the flow of abundance and it shows up as feelings of lack or worries like, 'There isn't enough.' Restoring warm Sacral energy is a truly positive way to get abundant energy flowing again.

SENSING THE SACRAL CHAKRA The Sacral Chakra sits at the
top of the triangular bone at the base of the spine, called the sacrum. In the diagram
above the Sacral Chakra can be seen as the orange circle in the lower back between
the hipbones. The Root Chakra is below it, at the level of the coccyx or tailbone.

As soon as you look at this diagram, one of the most familiar physical associations will be backache and lower back strain. These are some of the commonest physical signs of depleted energy in the Sacral and Root chakras; if the pain is slightly higher up between the hips, in the sacral area itself, then this definitely points to the Sacral Chakra.

Physical pain has physical causes

We need to remember that low energy in a chakra is not the cause of the pain; the pain is a sign from the body alerting you to the fact that something is not right. The original Indian healing system says the chakras are energetic, working as an extra dimension to the physical body. If there is a physical pain in the body,

it is likely that the chakra in that area is depleted; working to restore the chakra will help the physical body to recover, because restoring the energy helps to encourage the process of physical repair.

Dance yourself happy

Another sign of stuck Sacral Chakra energy is stiffness in the hips and lack of mobility; dancing is a great way to get the energy of the Sacral Chakra going again. A classic example of this is belly dancing, where the circular and figure-of-eight movements using the hips really work to release the energy in the hips. Latin American dances like salsa or samba also work really well to release the hips and bring a sense of joy. Sacral chakra energy is like that: warm, smiling and happy.

YOGA POSTURE FOR THE SACRAL CHAKRA

The posture we are going to use to open the Sacral Chakra is called Baddha Konasana, Bound Angle or Butterfly Pose. It opens the hips, eases out stiffness in the lower back and stretches the muscles inside the thighs. It is a good pose to do at the end of a long day, particularly if you have been sitting for long periods at a desk or doing a lot of driving.

1 *Sit on the floor with your legs stretched out straight in front of you. If you are uncomfortable you can place a low cushion under your bottom for support.*

2 *Take a slow breath in, and as you breathe out, bend your hips outwards and bring your knees to the sides, joining the soles of your feet together.*

3 *Bring your feet inwards as close to your pelvis as you can, without feeling pain in your knees. Go carefully and don't force it. Hold your feet with your hands.*

4 *Straighten your spine up from the hips, keep your shoulders relaxed, and gently move your knees up and down. This creates the 'butterfly': it's like a butterfly flexing its wings.*

5 *Pause in the posture for a few moments, then release the feet and straighten the legs. When you release the posture you may well feel a tingling in the legs and the lower back; this is a sign of energy moving in the area, as well as renewed circulation.*

SACRAL CHAKRA MEDITATION

As we have seen, some key words associated with the Sacral Chakra are 'flow' and 'abundance'. This meditation takes you on an inner journey to get in touch with these ideas again, and if possible to feel them on a sensory level. This stimulates the energy of the Sacral Chakra, opening you up to all the possibilities that want to flow into and through your life. The way to energize this chakra is to receive energy, to feel open and responsive. Water is the element associated with the Sacral Chakra; this is a wonderful symbol of flowing energy.

Sit on a firm-backed chair, or if you can sit cross-legged on the floor, with your spine upright, that is fine too. It's important to be comfortable. You may wish to record this meditation to listen to. It is also a lovely meditation to do in the shower.

Meditation

Imagine you are walking up a path on a warm summer's day. There are bright flowers everywhere, the sky is blue above your head: this is a beautiful place. Beside you is a sparkling stream, the water shining in the light as it flows in the direction you are walking. As you come around a bend, you see the stream flows into a pool, and at the other side of it is a small waterfall.

You are barefooted, and you walk into the water, feeling the soft coolness of it around your feet. You move to stand under the waterfall. The shower of the water is soothing on your skin; you feel it flow over the top of your head, down your shoulders and chest, over your hips, down your arms and legs and on into the pool. There is always more water flowing; it is endless. As you stand under the waterfall, you feel the movement of the water and the energy moves in and through you, nourishing your body and mind. All you have to do is receive it.

"Not what we have, but what we enjoy constitutes our abundance."
EPICURUS

OTHER SACRAL CHAKRA ENERGIZING IDEAS The
Sacral Chakra benefits hugely from movement. Exercise is often something that is done as a regime, out of duty or feelings of pressure, but learning to open up and move in whatever way you enjoy is a healthy way to re-energize the Sacral Chakra.

Get into the flow
Water is the element of the Sacral Chakra, so swimming is very beneficial. Breaststroke is particularly good to do for Sacral energy because of the movement of the legs, opening the hips out each time you do a stroke, before pushing the legs back to move you forward. Try and make your movements as smooth as possible as you swim; keep the idea of 'flow' in your mind, and remember the effortless movement of a fish. Wherever you swim, whether in the sea, a river or your local pool, enjoy yourself: never mind the fifty lengths, try swimming with energy awareness instead.

Open up your wardrobe

Another way of getting in touch with Sacral Chakra energy is to put aside the drab colours and restrictive workwear of the week and get out clothes with colour, patterns – clothes that you enjoy wearing. It might be a bright shirt for a man, or a flowing skirt for a woman – just something that spices up your energy and makes you feel good.

Creative expression

Sacral Chakra energy is also about getting into the flow of creativity and doing whatever you enjoy. Painting pictures, making jewellery, cooking for pleasure: the possibilities are endless. If you use your creativity to make things good for you and for those around you – being generous, reaching out to the people you care about – that is bringing in Sacral Chakra energy: remember, this chakra is about relationships. Cooking a fine meal for a group of friends and enjoying it together is a Sacral Chakra celebration.

SACRAL CHAKRA ENERGY TOOLS

Here we will look at two examples of tools you can use to enhance Sacral Chakra energy. If you are concentrating on re-energizing this chakra, these are elements you can incorporate into your everyday life to enhance the spiritual work that you are doing.

Amber

Amber is a kind of resin from pine trees that has fossilized over millions of years. It is typically found in beautiful 'teardrop' shapes, which make lovely beads, or larger pieces which are easily set in jewellery. Because it is a resin, it is wonderfully lightweight and feels warm against the skin. Its typical colour varies from golden yellow to deep warm orange; this is the shade that works best to energize the Sacral Chakra.

Amber is used in crystal healing to bring brightness and joy to the mind, to expand creative thinking and to revitalize the whole body. Wearing amber jewellery is a wonderful way to carry the energy of the Sacral Chakra with you during your day.

Sandalwood essential oil

The rich, warm woody smell of sandalwood essential oil (santalum album) from India is a classic scent to energize the Sacral Chakra. In Indian Ayurvedic medicine, sandalwood is used in massage as a tonic to re-energize and strengthen the body; it is also the base of many perfumes, while the wood is burned as incense. Indian sandalwood essential oil is expensive to buy because it is becoming rare, but it is worth the investment to use such a beautiful sacred aroma. Placing two drops onto a tissue on a windowsill, or in a fragrance burner, releases the aroma into the air. This is a wonderful fragrance to accompany the Sacral Chakra yoga pose and meditation, adding a sensory layer to those exercises.

KEY SACRAL CHAKRA ENERGY TOOLS

| SANDALWOOD OIL | AMBER | FLOW & ABUNDANCE |

The Solar Plexus Chakra: Introduction & Colour

The Solar Plexus Chakra is golden-yellow coloured, full of bright, shining energy like the sun. It is also a place of personal power; when it is fully activated, you literally 'shine your light' into the world. This is something many of us are not used to doing, either through lack of self-confidence or life events that have discouraged the development of personal power. When you see someone who is working on this level, there is a kind of aura around them when they enter a room.

Personal power does not mean arrogance, over-confidence, being big-headed or domineering over other people. These are signs that this chakra is being over-stimulated, which can have negative effects in the way others perceive you. The Solar Plexus Chakra symbolizes your unique gifts, what you have to offer the world, and gives you the confidence to let yourself be seen for who you really are. A simple affirmation for this chakra is 'I do'.

Being your best self

In the story of Cinderella, her fairy godmother turns her into a princess for the ball; ragged Cinderella is magically turned into a radiant and beautiful girl for all to see. When she runs away at midnight, it is because she is not quite ready to really be that princess for real – but she leaves her slipper behind, so that she can be found and brought back into that new world that truly waits for her.

The Solar Plexus Chakra has powerful energy and it is a chakra level which many people find challenging. The key thing is to embrace what it means, knowing that this chakra holds the key to bringing your unique gifts, talents and presence to the world.

SENSING THE SOLAR PLEXUS CHAKRA
The Solar Plexus Chakra is located under the curve between the ribs, just at the top of the stomach area, above the navel. If you find this place with your hand and press in slightly you may feel it is tender; this is quite normal because this is a vulnerable spot. A plexus is a place where nerve fibres come together in a bundle; there are many plexus spots in the body. This one happens to be at a chakra location, making it very sensitive.

The Sanskrit name for this chakra, Manipura, means 'jewel place', and its element is fire, showing that in the original map of the chakras, this energy level is a place of power. It's where you get the burst of energy that takes you into new places or new experiences in your life.

This is the chakra that governs the organs of the digestive system, liver and spleen, where the food we eat is converted into the energy we need to live. Digestive upsets like stomach aches, indigestion, heartburn or excess gas are physical signs that this chakra centre may need help. As well as looking after the physical signs, for example using soothing herbal teas, it is also helpful to do some energy exercises to support the Solar Plexus Chakra.

Finding your power

Mental signs of disturbance to the Solar Plexus Chakra include feeling overwhelmed or unable to act in situations where you face other people, feeling unable to stand up for yourself, feeling intimidated or inhibited from expressing your needs. All these situations show that the Solar Plexus Chakra needs re-energizing.

Working with this chakra may take some time, especially if these issues have been there for a while, but as you restore the Solar Plexus Chakra your sense of self-worth and self-confidence will return.

YOGA POSTURE FOR THE SOLAR PLEXUS CHAKRA

This posture, Ustrasana or Camel Pose, is excellent as a backward stretch for the upper and mid back; as you perform the pose, your chest and ribs open out, which opens the whole area of the Solar Plexus Chakra. When doing this pose, do not strain or try and push your body further than it wants to go. It's important to work with your body, and the more you practise, the more supple your back will be. For beginners, rest your hands where they feel comfortable, for example, on your hips.

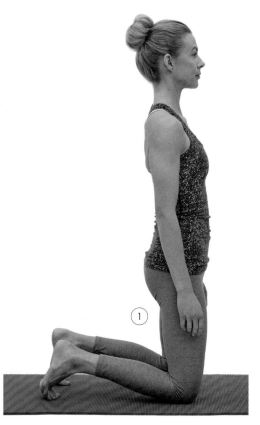

1 Start kneeling on your mat, your knees hip-width apart and your thighs perpendicular to the floor. Your feet should be bent with your toes touching the floor.

2 Rest your hands on your hips and gently push them forwards; push out your chest and shoulders, slowly leaning backwards. Do not force this movement. You will feel a strong stretch up the front of your thighs. Try and keep your neck relaxed and don't hunch your shoulders.

3 If you can, extend your hands down towards your feet; eventually you will be able to touch them, but don't force this movement, only go as far as you feel comfortable. Go back as far as you can and hold the pose for up to a minute.

4 Slowly come back up to kneel, then relax forwards into Child's Pose to recover for a few minutes.

Health Benefits

This posture benefits all the organs of the abdomen; it also opens up the chest and hips, improving the flexibility of the middle of the back.

SOLAR PLEXUS CHAKRA MEDITATION
As we have seen, the Solar Plexus Chakra is a place of powerful, bright energy. Using this visualization can help you to get used to the intensity of its vibration, working with it so you feel comfortable with its level and understanding how it feels when it increases and decreases.

Find a quiet space; sit on a firm-backed chair with your legs uncrossed and your feet on the floor. You can also sit on the floor cross-legged if that is comfortable for you.

You may wish to record this visualization to listen to.

First, sit quietly and breathe comfortably for a few moments. Feel your body supported by the chair but don't sag into it; sit poised in the chair, your spine upright. If you are sitting on the floor, concentrate on lifting your spine out of the cradle of your hips.

Place your hands over the Solar Plexus Chakra in the middle of your abdomen, just under your ribs. Breathe in deeply; feel the abdomen and chest expand as you do so. Breathe out, and feel your hands move inwards as the chest contracts.

Concentrate on your hands. Imagine that your hands are filling with bright golden energy, and as you breathe in slowly, imagine that energy is filling the Solar Plexus Chakra. As you breathe out, that golden energy spreads into the chest, stomach and upper abdomen, warm, tingling, golden and bright. Repeat this a few times.

Now imagine that your hands are receiving even brighter golden energy; it's getting stronger, like brilliant sunlight. Breathe in and receive it into the Solar Plexus Chakra; breathe out and let it permeate the chest and upper abdomen. Repeat this a few times, feeling the higher intensity.

Now return to the less intense golden energy, still bright, still beautiful. Breathe it into your Solar Plexus Chakra, breathe it out into the body.

Rest your hands in your lap. Sit quietly for a few moments, noticing how the energy feels in your Solar Plexus Chakra.

"I am not afraid of tomorrow for I have
seen yesterday and I love today."
WILLIAM ALLEN WHITE

OTHER SOLAR PLEXUS CHAKRA ENERGIZING IDEAS

The most obvious way to energize the Solar Plexus Chakra is to spend time outdoors in the sunshine. The media is full of warnings about over-exposing the skin to UV rays, which is wise advice, especially if your skin is pale or very sensitive. However, here we are not talking about sunbathing, but more about general exposure to sunlight. This is very beneficial and we need it in order to manufacture Vitamin D, vital to the immune system and to bone health.

Owning your power

Starting a new project or learning a new skill is also good for this chakra – going beyond thinking about doing it and actually doing it, especially if it takes a bit of a leap of faith or challenges you. Yes, there might be a bit of nervousness in the pit of your stomach where the Solar Plexus Chakra lives, but the feeling when you overcome the nerves and actually do it is when this chakra really comes to life.

The light of others

Another way to energize the Solar Plexus Chakra is to spend some time with people who really love what they do, whatever that may be. Whether it's conservation of beautiful places, amateur theatrics, singing with a choir, or watching the work of artists or craftspeople, the key thing is, the energy that you perceive, the happiness and enjoyment that people are experiencing, is infectious. It picks you up and carries you along, and that's good for the Solar Plexus Chakra. Laughter is good for it too.

Spending time outdoors

Spending time walking or gardening or eating outdoors are activities where moderate exposure to sunlight creates a feeling of wellbeing. Human beings originally lived outside, hunting and gathering all that they needed to exist. Nowadays many of us get up, drive to work or get the train, stay inside while we work and travel home again, barely going outside at all. In the long term, this is not beneficial: going out into broad spectrum daylight, especially in the middle of the day, is vital for brain health, and also helps relieve stress.

SOLAR PLEXUS CHAKRA ENERGY TOOLS At this point we'll

discuss two special tools that you can use to enhance Solar Plexus Chakra energy in your everyday life. Working with these tools enhances the exercises in previous pages, helping to restore and re-energize your body and mind.

Citrine

Citrine is a beautiful golden quartz with a lovely sparkling energy. It is important when you buy this crystal to make sure it is genuine citrine, which a good supplier should be able to guarantee; sometimes very yellow quartz stones are actually heat-treated amethyst. Natural citrine has a lovely pale yet clear colour.

Citrine is used in crystal healing to balance and nourish the Solar Plexus Chakra. A simple way to experience this is to lie down and place a citrine crystal on your upper abdomen in the area of the Solar Plexus Chakra. Breathe gently and absorb the clear golden energy.

Carrying a citrine crystal with you during your day in your bag or in a pocket enables you to hold it whenever you need a boost of Solar Plexus Chakra energy. Citrine is also used in crystal jewellery, so wearing it is another way to feel energized and strengthened.

Lemon essential oil

Lemon essential oil is pressed from lemon peel. If you pare a little rind off a lemon and turn it upside down you can see tiny sacs in the peel; press these with your nail and the sharp, fresh, bright aroma of lemon zest is instantly there with you. The best lemon essential oil comes from Sicily, where the fruit swells and ripens under the glorious Mediterranean sun.

Try putting four drops of lemon essential oil into a fragrance burner or onto a tissue on the windowsill; the sharp aroma instantly refreshes the air and lifts the spirits. In aromatherapy lemon essential oil is used to stimulate and detoxify the body; its mouth-watering scent stimulates the digestion. Coming from the bright yellow fruit, this essential oil is a perfect tonic for the Solar Plexus Chakra.

KEY SOLAR PLEXUS CHAKRA ENERGY TOOLS

LEMON OIL	CITRINE	BRIGHT ENERGY

67

The Heart Chakra: Introduction & Colour

The Heart Chakra sits right in the middle of the chest, at the level of the breastbone. It is the point of balance of the seven chakras, with three below it and three above. Sometimes the three lower chakras are described as being more 'earth based', meaning linked to physical life, while the three upper chakras are described as being more 'spiritual', meaning they are linked to mental, inspirational and spiritual aspects of being. The Heart Chakra sits in the centre, joining earth to spirit, nourished by the more physical chakras and inspired by those above it.

The colour of the Heart Chakra is a vibrant green, like rich, abundant leaves. Green is a colour combination of yellow (the colour of the Solar Plexus Chakra, just below) and blue (the colour of the Throat Chakra, just above); again, it is a point of balance between these particular chakra colours. Green is the energy of growth, vitality, opening; think of the marvellous display of spring, where the dull branches of winter burst suddenly into life.

Green energy

In medieval times, the German saint, mystic and scholar Hildegard of Bingen (1098–1179) wrote about the power of what she called viriditas, which literally means 'greening'. She saw it as life-giving, fertile and rich energy, symbolizing everlasting life.

'Green' has another powerful meaning today, linked to ecology, earth conservation and living with an understanding of humankind's effect on the Earth. On a very practical level, activities like recycling and living sustainably are Heart Chakra-centred, for the benefit of the planet itself.

A simple affirmation for the heart chakra is 'I love.' This is not sexual passion or the mad rush of falling in love; it is unconditional love, or compassion for all living things.

SENSING THE HEART CHAKRA
The Heart Chakra sits over the breastbone in the centre of the chest, which is a common place of emotional tension. Although the energy of love that it truly represents is unconditional, because it sits in that central point of balance, it can easily be affected by issues arising from other chakras. For example, overwhelming passionate feelings from the Sacral Chakra, the sexual centre, can translate as a rush of expanding energy in the heart. However, since such passion rarely lasts, it is in the Heart Chakra that loss, grief and heartbreak can actually feel like physical pain. Another example might be Solar Plexus-related, perhaps the sudden loss of a job, affecting your own self-esteem: you might well feel sadness in the Heart Chakra, especially if you 'put your heart' into what you do.

The Heart Chakra can also become very depleted in anyone who spends most of their time giving to other people. Parents are the prime example: they can become exhausted and depleted by the demands of nurturing children. Nurses, teachers, social workers, holistic therapists, carers: working in these kinds of fields requires you to give, to care, to nurture, to support, which are all aspects of Heart Chakra energy. However, if you keep giving without replenishing your energy, the end result can be 'burnout'.

Preserving your heart
If this sounds like you (and many people are in this situation), it is important to stop, breathe and spend some time allowing your Heart Chakra to be replenished. This chakra needs to receive energy as well as providing it. A very simple thing to do is to step out into nature and allow yourself to absorb its green, nurturing beauty, even for a few moments.

YOGA POSTURE FOR THE HEART CHAKRA Here we are

looking at a slight variation on a traditional yoga pose called Cobra (Bhujangasana); this pose is called the Sphinx (Salamba Bhujangasana). The Sphinx Pose is easier for beginners in yoga because the weight of the torso is supported on the forearms, so the bend in the back is not as extreme as it is in Cobra. However, the Sphinx Pose still opens the chest and benefits the area of the Heart Chakra.

1 *Start by lying down on your mat with your arms bent by your sides and your palms flat on the floor by your shoulders. Breathe slowly and calmly.*

2 *Breathe in, and on the out breath, push up gently with your arms so that your upper arms are perpendicular to the floor. Lift up your chest, and let your neck rise*

up out of your shoulders. Look straight forward. As you breathe, be aware of your Heart Chakra and imagine on the in-breath that it is receiving life-giving energy.

①

②

Take Care of Yourself

With a little practice, you will find it easier to hold the Sphinx Pose for longer. In the beginning, do not strain: hold it as long as you feel is best for your body.

If you have any lower back pain or strain, or if you are pregnant, this pose is not advised. It's always worth consulting a doctor if you're not sure if a pose is safe.

3 *As you hold the pose you will feel a stretch all down your back; instinctively you will clench your buttocks, but try not to do this too hard. Keep your legs straight.*

4 *Hold the pose for at least thirty seconds, then lower back down to the floor and lie there with your head on one side.*

5 *As a counter-stretch, it is good to move into Child's Pose.*

④

⑤

HEART CHAKRA MEDITATION

This meditation for the Heart Chakra is a standing sequence with movements attuned to the breath. If you can do this sequence outside it is even more beneficial, breathing fresh air and standing on the earth. Whether you are inside or outside, it is best done barefoot, because your feet need to feel a direct connection to the earth.

Stand comfortably, your feet shoulder-width apart. Start with your hands together over your heart in a 'prayer position'. As you stand like this, begin to take slow, regular breaths, in and out. In your mind, let this thought be your focus: 'I stand balanced between Earth and heaven.' Really feel the connection between your feet and the ground; sense the difference between that solid connection and the wider space around your head.

Breathe in and spread your arms wide, so they are perpendicular to the ground. Let this thought be in your mind: 'I open to receive love from nature.' Feel the expansion of your Heart Chakra; as you breathe in and out, visualize it filling with vibrant green life-giving energy.

On an in-breath, raise your arms above your head. As you do this, let this thought be in your mind: 'I open to receive love from the universe.' Pause here, breathing gently, for a moment.

Breathe in and return your hands to the starting position over your heart. Let this thought be in your mind: 'I radiate boundless love to the entire world.' As your hands rest over your Heart Chakra, feel the difference in its energy now: as you are filled, you have even more energy to share with the world.

Repeat this sequence slowly three times, with awareness, and notice how you feel when you have finished.

*"Radiate boundless love towards
the entire world"*
THE BUDDHA

OTHER HEART CHAKRA ENERGIZING IDEAS

The Heart Chakra is one that needs to receive energy. When we think about 'energizing', we tend to think that means doing something active, which of course is often true. However, it is possible to re-energize by just being aware, receptive and open. This is a concept that may sound strange, especially when so much of life is spent doing things, yet practising 'being' is a wonderful way to enable the Heart Chakra to be restored.

Expand your senses

A simple way to practise 'being' is to use your senses in a truly conscious way. Most of the time, the senses of sight, hearing, touch, taste and smell are just taken for granted as we move through our day. However, pausing to appreciate our senses for the wonderful gifts of sensations they give us all the time is a wonderful way to nourish the Heart Chakra.

Awareness exercise

The next time you go to a place you particularly love, stop there for a while and find a comfortable place to sit. Relax, and breathe calmly. Let your eyes slowly take in the whole scene in front of you. Let the shapes, colours, features and people if they are there, all be absorbed into your awareness.

Now be aware of the sounds in the place. Let these sounds come into your awareness. As you tune into them, you may find new sounds that you have not heard before.

Now be aware of how you sit, where you sit, how your body responds to being in that place.

Finally, notice any aromas in the air: scents of nature, scents of the environment, scents that are familiar, or any that are new.

Then sit and let all this sensory information fill you in this place that you love. Be thankful for the senses that allow you to appreciate it.

Feeling gratitude is one of the best ways to restore the Heart Chakra.

HEART CHAKRA ENERGY TOOLS

Here we will consider two special energy tools to use in daily life to nourish and support the Heart Chakra. In holistic healing, this chakra is associated with the colour pink, as a symbol of unconditional love. A beautiful pink rose with rich green Heart Chakra-coloured leaves is a lovely symbol of these two colours working together.

Rose quartz

In crystal healing, the Heart Chakra can be energized either by green or pink stones. Rose quartz is a beautiful soft pink crystal with a gentle, radiating energy. It can be bought as small polished tumblestones, unpolished pieces or polished points or 'wands'. It is also very popular set in silver crystal jewellery.

Wearing rose quartz in a pendant, for example, is a wonderful way to carry that Heart Chakra energy with you during your day. In any moments of stress or tension, just holding the pendant for a few moments can calm your heart and mind.

Rose essential oil

The beautiful damask rose, Rosa damascena, shows the pink and green colours of the Heart Chakra together. It is a 'perfume rose' with a rich soft sweet scent coming from the essential oil in the flower. Rose essential oil is incredibly costly to extract: it takes about two hundred flowers to release one drop. Fortunately it is possible to buy rose essential oil diluted in jojoba oil to use as a more affordable and beautiful natural skin perfume.

Dabbing a little rose in jojoba onto your chest in the area of the Heart Chakra is a beautiful way to nourish its energy. The warm sweet aroma soothes your senses and calms your emotions.

KEY HEART CHAKRA ENERGY TOOLS

ROSE OIL	ROSE QUARTZ	ATTUNE TO BREATH

The Throat Chakra: Introduction & Colour

The Throat Chakra has a light blue colour, like the clear shining hue of a summer sky. It energy is expansive, creative and positive, the energy of communication using the voice, whether in speaking, singing or chanting. In Buddhist and Hindu traditions, the Throat Chakra is energized by chanting 'mantras', which are very ancient words spoken or sung in a particular pattern, repeated many times. The vibration of sound passing through the Throat Chakra bathes and supports all of the chakras in turn. One of the most famous mantras is 'Om mani padme hum', which is difficult to translate directly into English: it speaks of transforming suffering and affirming the presence of universal energy with the spirit of pure wisdom and compassion.

A simple affirmation for the Throat Chakra is 'I speak.' The power of the voice is amazing; even in simple conversation, the words we say aloud can uplift or deplete other people. The voice is an aspect of human life that we take totally for granted, and yet it represents a part of life that can change everything. Words spoken in anger or designed to hurt someone can totally disrupt a relationship. Positive words of encouragement can console someone who is depressed, reminding them that they are not alone. The quality of the energy being transmitted through the voice, positive or negative, is powerful.

Singing is an aspect of voice that directly benefits the brain, making you feel light-hearted; choral groups feel this effect when they sing together. The Throat Chakra and the Heart Chakra have a unique connection; consider, for instance, how often they are united in love songs. If the music moves you, if you feel the emotion of it, the song and the singer have done their work.

SENSING THE THROAT CHAKRA The Throat Chakra is located
at the base of the throat, at the level of the slight indentation; if you place your fingers gently at the base of the throat and speak, it's just below where your voicebox is.

The Throat Chakra is very affected by feelings and emotions. Sometimes you might feel 'choked' because someone has said something to you that has upset you; or you might feel your throat is constricted because you are experiencing strong emotions you can't express. If you are faced with someone who intimidates you, you might feel tightness in your Throat Chakra as you try to speak your truth. If during your lifetime you have felt unable to really say what you want to say – and this can build up as deep resentment over many years – the Throat Chakra will definitely be very depleted.

The ache of silence

Other manifestations of low Throat Chakra energy are persistent sore throats, throat infections or neck pain; maybe someone in your life is, literally, a pain in the neck.

The Throat Chakra is not the cause of these conditions: it is simply reacting to their physical effects on the body.

The good news is, there are many ways to replenish, restore and strengthen Throat Chakra energy. Regular practice can also benefit the whole chakra system, improving your energy vibration when you go out into the world and communicate with other people. The more you speak from the heart, telling your truth clearly, the more you attract beneficial and positive energy into your life.

YOGA POSTURE FOR THE THROAT CHAKRA The Throat

Chakra can often feel constricted or closed. This yoga posture, Matsyasana or the Fish, is a wonderful opening movement, not just for the Throat Chakra but also for the Heart Chakra as well. There are many variations to this posture, but this simple version is suitable for beginners.

Watch Your Back

Sometimes in a class with a yoga teacher, cushions or bolsters are placed behind the back to support a deeper arching backward stretch. If you are a beginner, start with this simple pose and work with a teacher to deepen it in the best way that suits your flexibility.

1 *Sit upright on your mat on the floor with your legs straight in front of you, ankles and feet together.*

2 *Slowly lean back and bend your arms on either side with your palms flat on the floor, to keep your chest at an angle.*

3 *On an out breath, push your chest forwards and lean your head back, still pushing down on your arms to keep you balanced. Don't force the head back any further than it wants to go. The aim is to eventually let the head rest lightly on the floor, but beginners will not usually be this supple.*

1

4 *Feel the sense of opening in your throat. As you breathe, imagine pale blue energy filling your Throat Chakra.*

5 *Hold the pose as long as you feel comfortable, then slowly lower yourself to the ground. Your spine should settle very comfortably on the mat. Breathe gently and rest for a few moments.*

②

③

⑤

THROAT CHAKRA MEDITATION

This is a sound exercise, designed to help you feel different vibrations passing through the Throat Chakra while opening the chest and the voice. Don't worry about 'being a singer' or 'being able to sing': this exercise lets you find your own pitch to make sound at whatever level is comfortable to you. If you have not used your voice like this for a long time, the sound you make may not be very strong; that is fine. With practice, you will become more confident.

Making sound in a concentrated way is a form of meditation; this method concentrates on the five vowel sounds. Notice, as you pronounce them, the way your mouth changes shape, and feel the effect of the vowel sound in your Throat Chakra.

Sit comfortably on a firm-backed chair, feet uncrossed, hands relaxed in your lap.

First, say out loud, 'AHH' (to rhyme with 'spa'). Feel this sound in your throat. Then, find a comfortable note and sing the sound AHH. Try this three times.

Second, say out loud, 'EHH' (to rhyme with 'chair'). Feel this sound in your throat. Then, on your comfortable note, sing the sound EHH three times.

Third, say out loud, 'EEH' (to rhyme with 'tree'). Feel this sound in your throat. Then, on your comfortable note, sing the sound EEH three times.

Fourth, say out loud, 'OHH' (to rhyme with 'toe'). Feel this sound in your throat. Then, on your comfortable note, sing the sound OHH three times.

Fifth, say out loud, 'OOH' (to rhyme with 'truth'). Feel this sound in your throat. Then, on your comfortable note, sing the sound OOH three times.

Now, join all five sounds in sequence: AHH, EHH, EEH, OHH, OOH. See if you can sound all five tones on one breath. Don't worry if you can't, just take breath where you need to.

Toning like this opens your Throat Chakra, and you may find it also clears your head. Later on pages 168–175 you will find more sound meditation exercises to try.

*"Let your tongue speak what
your heart thinks."*
DAVY CROCKETT.

OTHER THROAT CHAKRA ENERGIZING IDEAS The

Throat Chakra can be nourished and supported by focusing on blue, its special colour. If you open the curtains in the morning and see an azure sky, open a window or go outside; take a few moments to breathe and absorb that wide, expansive energy, then feel it bathing and restoring your Throat Chakra. Pale blue is a gentle, peaceful colour, cooling and soothing to the mind and the emotions, wide and clear as the heavens.

Positive communication

Another way to energize the Throat Chakra is to exercise your favourite form of communication. This may be through the voice, in acting, singing or public speaking, or even telling jokes. It may also be through the written word, through writing a journal, poetry or fiction or positive affirmations to inspire you.

Releasing your truth

If you have strong emotions and feelings that you just can't communicate directly, you can use this simple healing ritual to release them to the earth. Simply write down the things you want to say; let them come out on paper. As you do this, know that you are just releasing this stuck energy so it doesn't stay inside you.

Once you have written your piece, screw the paper into a ball, take it outside, place it on the earth and set it alight with a match. (Choose a safe place to do this well away from anything flammable.) When the paper has burned up, dig the ashes into the earth, which has wonderful neutralizing energy. Doing this with a positive intention is very empowering; sometimes this ritual can actually change the situation for the better, because you go back to the person concerned with a different attitude. This releasing ritual is very beneficial to the Throat Chakra: by releasing your emotions, you are freed to speak your truth.

THROAT CHAKRA ENERGY TOOLS These are two special
energy tools to help support and energize the Throat Chakra as you move through
everyday life.

Blue lace agate

This beautiful pale blue stone is an agate,
a form of microcrystalline quartz; it forms
in layers with bands of slightly different
shades running through it, like pale blue
or white. When it is polished, it has a
soft, gentle blue appearance. It is a good
stone to carry with you; hold it to remind
you of the presence of the Throat Chakra
and to focus on its energy. Wearing a
pendant with a blue lace agate stone is
another way to feel your Throat Chakra
is replenished as you go through your
day. It is particularly good to do this if
you are going into situations where you
feel you need extra support to speak.

Roman chamomile essential oil

The daisy-like flowers of Roman chamomile
(Anthemis nobilis) release an essential oil
through distillation that has a delicate
pale blue colour due to a constituent
called azulene. This makes the essential
oil soothing and slightly anti-inflammatory
when it is used on the skin.

The scent of Roman chamomile is very
light, sweet and sharp, with fruity, apple-
like notes. It is a very calming and gentle
essential oil, often used in blends or
products for children. Put four drops of
Roman chamomile essential oil into a
vaporizer or on a tissue on the windowsill
to enjoy its light, soft aroma.

Later, on pages 144–149, you will
find out how to make a blend to use this
essential oil safely on your skin. Applying
your blend on the area of your Throat
Chakra before you go to sleep helps to
restore its energy while you rest.

KEY THROAT CHAKRA ENERGY TOOLS

ROMAN CHAMOMILE OIL	BLUE LACE AGATE	SOUND

The Third Eye Chakra: Introduction & Colour

The Third Eye Chakra is a mystical energy centre, positioned between the eyebrows. It is the first of two more deeply spiritual chakras, the second one being the Crown Chakra. Both are extremely sensitive and represent higher levels of consciousness.

What does 'higher levels of consciousness' mean? We have seen that the first three chakras (Root, Sacral and Solar Plexus) govern some of the most important physical systems of the body, like the digestive or urinary or nervous systems. The next two chakras (Heart and Throat) link to feelings and communication. The final two chakras in the seven chakra energy system, Third Eye and Crown, open the possibility of higher expressions of human life, such as creativity, inspiration and healing.

A place of insight

The Third Eye is named Ajna in Sanskrit, which means 'to command' or 'to perceive'. It is a higher way of seeing than the eyes themselves, linking it to intuition, a sixth sense or a deep inner knowing beyond the logic of the mind. A simple affirmation for it is 'I see', but remember this seeing is beyond normal vision. Sensations like déjà vu – being somewhere and knowing it although you think you have never been in that place before – may well be a sign from the Third Eye Chakra.

Deep perception

The colour of the Third Eye Chakra is indigo blue, the dark, rich colour of the night sky. Going outside on a clear evening and looking up at a star-scattered firmament, allowing it to bathe your mind and senses, is a very simple and beautiful way to restore your Third Eye Chakra.

Working with this chakra opens up creative thinking in your brain, helping to offer you solutions to problems that might surprise you. Third Eye Chakra energy is not logical or methodical; it is inspirational, unusual and spontaneous. When you get an idea and it means taking a leap of faith, but a deep knowing says 'do it anyway', this is a gift from the Third Eye Chakra.

SENSING THE THIRD EYE CHAKRA The Third Eye Chakra's
position between the eyebrows links it closely to the eyes themselves; its indigo blue
colour and energy are soothing and supportive to their health and physical function.

When the eyes are irritated and sore from straining to read or working on a computer for hours, it is very beneficial to use Third Eye Chakra exercises to calm and restore them. Sitting in meditation and visualizing the eyes and the forehead bathed in the indigo blue colour is a simple way to start.

Life's headaches

Mental stress and overload, tension headaches and feelings of pressure are very common issues in daily life. Feeling as though your head is going to explode, trying to take in too much information at one time, feeling exam or work pressure; these problems all manifest in this area of the face and head. The signs of physical discomfort all point to the Third Eye Chakra and its need for restoration and healing.

Take time out

The more depleted the Third Eye Chakra becomes, the more mental stress starts to feel like overload. In the social-media-mad world we live in, where people walk around constantly linked to their mobile phones, mental stress is everywhere. This may feel like a big effort, but when you get home tonight, just for a while, try switching off all electronic devices and make time to be quiet. It is important to break the cycle. The best nourishment for the Third Eye Chakra is peace.

You will begin to notice that as you practise giving yourself these times of quiet, your ability to cope with mental stress improves and the energy in your Third Eye Chakra is restored.

YOGA POSTURE FOR THE THIRD EYE CHAKRA The Third

Eye Chakra benefits from many different positions in yoga. This asana called Downward Facing Dog (Adho Mukha Svanasana) is one of the most beneficial; it works as a wonderful all-over body tonic, particularly nourishing to the spine and the Third Eye Chakra. Take note that this is an inverted pose with the head upside down, so as a beginner it is best to hold this pose only as long as you feel comfortable.

1 *Start by kneeling down on all fours on your mat. Your thighs need to be parallel to the floor, your arms straight but not locked, your palms directly beneath your shoulders.*

2 *Spread your hands on the mat so your middle finger is pointing straight ahead. Lift your heels and curl your toes under your feet, facing forwards.*

3 *Push down on your hands and lift your hips upwards, stretching your spine, keeping your knees bent at the moment. Your head, neck and spine should be all be in line.*

4 If you can, flatten your feet and stretch your legs out fully, planting your feet firmly on the ground. Feel the stretch up the back of your legs, the power of your arms holding you up.

5 As you hold the posture for a few moments, feel the energy running down your spine and into your Third Eye Chakra.

6 Release by coming back down onto all fours.

7 Move into Child's Pose to rest.

THIRD EYE CHAKRA MEDITATION

The Third Eye Chakra benefits from this gentle meditation, especially at the end of a long busy day. For a while, put aside everything that distracts you and focus on replenishing yourself.

Sit comfortably on a firm-backed chair. Place your feet flat on the floor, relax your hands in your lap and sit up straight. If you like, you can light a stick of incense to inhale the aroma as you meditate. It may help to record this meditation to listen to as you sit.

Close your eyes and take a few slow, deep breaths. Feel the support of the chair beneath you. Let the worries of your day dissolve away. Focus on your breathing, in and out, for a few moments.

Now imagine you are standing on the edge of a lake. It is night time, but you can see the water rippling gently away from you towards the horizon. Above you is a vast, deep blue night sky, patterned with millions of stars twinkling like tiny diamonds. Breathe in the deep, cool indigo colour into your forehead, bathing your eyes, flowing into and nourishing your Third Eye Chakra.

As you look back at the lake and its dark blue shimmer before you, a beautiful full moon rises slowly into the sky. Its light makes a pattern of reflections on the water. Let the rippling light of these reflections bathe your mind, soothing away anxieties and daily cares.

Take a slow, deep breath and say 'I come back to the present moment and touch life deeply. This is mindfulness.'

Open your eyes and sit quietly for a few moments. Notice how you feel.

*"Do not lose yourself in the past.
Do not lose yourself in the future. Do not get
caught in your anger, worries or fears. Come back
to the present moment and touch life deeply.
This is mindfulness."*

THICH NHAT HANH

OTHER THIRD EYE CHAKRA ENERGIZING IDEAS The
Third Eye Chakra has a higher sensory energy, giving impressions of things that are beyond the logical mind. Practising energy sensing is an interesting and fun way to increase your awareness of a different dimension to everyday activity.

Energy in your hands

Rub your palms together briskly for a few moments until they start to feel really warm. Then move your hands about two feet apart, holding them parallel. Close your eyes. Bring your palms closer together, slowly, until you feel a tingling sensation between them. Open your eyes and notice how far apart they are. Rub your hands together again, and repeat the exercise. Do this a few times. What you may begin to notice is that your hands are further apart each time, but you can still feel the energy between them, that tingling warmth.

Energy in crystals

You can also practise energy sensing holding a crystal. Choose a stone you particularly like and sit in your meditation position on your chair, holding

it in your cupped hands. Relax and breathe; let your awareness flow into the crystal, and see what happens. Try not to think about what kind of crystal it is; simply be aware of it in your hands. You may feel energy from it, or feel your hands tingle: these are both signs of intuition from the Third Eye Chakra.

Energy in nature

You can do this exercise with a selection of flowers blooming in different colours. Find some bright red blooms to start with; hold your hands over them a few inches away, and see what you sense. Then repeat this with some blue flowers as a contrast. Then try with some yellow ones. The energy you feel each time may well be different. The more you practise this, the more different colours will give you different sensations. This is a useful practice linking to colour healing.

THIRD EYE CHAKRA ENERGY TOOLS Here, we'll cover two

special tools that can be used alongside the other exercises in this section to enhance your Third Eye Chakra work.

Lapis lazuli crystal

Lapis lazuli is a stunning stone with a rich deep blue colour, made even more vivid when it is polished; it also has tiny gold flecks in it that are pyrite grains. It has been considered to be a sacred stone for thousands of years. In Ancient Egypt, lapis lazuli was worn in crowns, collars and jewellery by the pharaohs; a famous example is Tutankhamun's gold neck collar, inlaid with lapis lazuli, onyx and carnelian. In crystal healing, lapis is often placed over the Third Eye Chakra to balance and restore its energies. You can try this for yourself, or practise energy sensing holding a lapis stone in your hands to restore your Third Eye Chakra. Wearing lapis lazuli as a pendant or earrings is an excellent way to keep this chakra energized during the day.

Frankincense essential oil

Frankincense essential oil comes from resin that oozes out of the bark of tough desert shrubs found in Somalia and Oman. The raw resin can be burned as incense, releasing a rich, heady-scented smoke. Distillation of ground resin releases the essential oil: the aroma of the resin in liquid form. The fragrance is rich, warm, sweet and fresh. Frankincense is a classic essential oil to burn for meditation; it helps calm the mind and bring a sense of inner peace and tranquillity. Try putting four drops of frankincense essential oil into a fragrance burner or onto a tissue on a windowsill to enjoy this deep, ancient aroma. This is a good thing to do as a background to practising other exercises from this Third Eye section.

KEY THIRD EYE CHAKRA ENERGY TOOLS

FRANKINCENSE OIL	LAPIS LAZULI	REPLENISHMENT

The Crown Chakra: Introduction & Colour

The Crown Chakra is seen as either purple in colour (the highest vibration in the rainbow colour spectrum), or pure white. In Sanskrit its name Sahasrara means 'thousand-petalled'; this refers to the image of the beautiful white lotus flower representing the highest level of consciousness.

We can use the example of the lotus flower to illustrate the Crown Chakra more clearly. The lotus likes to grow in a pool of water. Its roots (Root Chakra) sink deep into the mud at the base of the pool, where they draw in physical nourishment from the earth. This nourishment encourages the upward growth of the stem (Sacral Chakra) and lower branches (Solar Plexus Chakra). At the level of the water, the midway point, the leaves spread out as a platform (Heart Chakra) and the flower bud forms. The flower is the highest expression of the plant (Throat Chakra); under the light of the cosmic sun, the bud begins to open (Third Eye Chakra) and the flower finally opens to full bloom, full consciousness (Crown Chakra). The fragrance of the flower, released beyond the physical form of the plant, is its highest creative expression: its spirit.

Natural blossoming

The lotus flower does not have to try and do any of this. All the amazing processes of upward growth, leaf expansion, preparation of the flower and blooming are in its DNA. Nourishment, water and light complete the process.

We can take this example into our lives. Each and every one of us has a seed of potential inside us. No matter where we live or what our circumstances, this seed is within us. By working with all the chakras, we can begin to open and sense this potential, feeling its energy. Finally by experiencing the energy of the Crown Chakra, we grow and flower, bringing our unique potential into the world. A simple affirmation for this chakra is 'I am'.

SENSING THE CROWN CHAKRA
The exact location of the Crown Chakra is on the top of the head. When a baby is born, its skull is not fully solid; the bones of the skull have to have some give in them to allow the baby to pass through the birth canal. As a result, its skull has soft membranes between the bones called fontanelles. The biggest of these, the anterior fontanelle, shows up clearly on many babies' heads. This is the location of the Crown Chakra. In adults, this place feels like a slight indentation in the middle of the top of your head.

The Crown Chakra governs the head and the brain within it; all the many processes and workings of the brain are affected. The pineal gland, a small gland deep in the core of the brain, is strongly associated with the Crown Chakra because it produces melatonin, the hormone associated with sleeping and waking, which are different states of consciousness. The experience of consciousness on all levels is the role of the Crown Chakra.

Resting your spirit
If you have problems sleeping, troubled sleep, disturbed dreams or irregular sleeping and waking patterns, these are signs the Crown Chakra may be depleted. Conditions like depression or anxiety or other psychological problems also indicate that the Crown Chakra may be out of balance. As we have seen before, the chakras are not the cause of these problems, and working with chakra energy is not a guaranteed cure for them either. However, using gentle tools and simple healing methods to improve the energy balance in the Crown Chakra is a good way to support a personal healing process.

If you feel you are in a state of mental discomfort or anxiety, it is always wise to consult a doctor or a counsellor for guidance, and to discuss your wish to use the tools and methods on the following pages.

YOGA POSTURE FOR THE CROWN CHAKRA Many

yoga positions support and restore the Crown Chakra; one of the most well-known is the Headstand (Shirshasana), but this is a challenging pose that is best demonstrated by a teacher. For beginners, an easy yoga position to use is the Seated Forward Bend (Paschimothanasana). This position provides a deep stretch to the spine, massages the digestive organs and opens the way for energy to flow into the Crown Chakra.

1 *Sit down on your mat on the floor with your legs straight out in front of you. Slide your hands under your bottom and pull your buttocks back slightly to make sure your hips are perpendicular. Sit up straight, rising out of the pelvis.*

2 *Stretch your arms up vertically, feeling the stretch all the way up your spine.*

3 Inhale, draw in your abdomen and the muscles in your core, exhale and lean forwards from the pelvis, keeping your back straight.

4 Lean your chest towards your thighs. Try not to arch the middle back. Let your hands rest on your legs at a comfortable level. Let your neck and shoulders relax.

5 The aim is to rest your forehead on your legs; however for beginners this may not be possible. If you like you can use a cushion on your knees to rest your head.

6 Hold the position for a few moments. Every time you breathe out, try and ease a little bit further forwards and down. Sense the energy in your spine, and visualize it running all the way to the Crown Chakra at the top of your head.

7 To ease out of the pose, bend your arms and support yourself back up to the first sitting position.

8 Finally, lie down on the floor to rest for a few moments.

109

CROWN CHAKRA MEDITATION

All forms of meditation benefit the Crown Chakra; the practice of meditation itself is intended to achieve inner peace and awareness. This is not something to be forced, or to be seen as an objective; it is not about trying or making an effort. It is about being. Many simple meditation techniques can help to settle the mind, relax the body and allow the spirit (Crown Chakra) to be nourished. This is a simple example.

This meditation is best done in the evening. You need to set up a small table in front of you, where you will place a candle or a tea light in a holder and light it. (Make sure your candle is placed well away from any flammable materials.) Sit comfortably on a firm-backed chair, or on the floor cross-legged if you prefer. Breathe deeply and feel your body relaxed but poised in your seated position. Allow yourself to feel quiet and at peace.

There is no other light in the room apart from the candle. Be aware of the dim light of the space around you, soft and soothing. Move your gaze to the little flame and watch it. That is all. If you find thoughts of your day intruding, just mentally blow them away like feathers on the wind. Keep gently bringing your eyes back to the little flame.

This flame is the symbol of the seed inside you. This flame is the spark of your creativity, the light that is you. This flame is a tiny part of a much greater light, the light of the sun; the light of the sun is connected to the light that is you. Just be with the light. Feel this light bathing and restoring your Crown Chakra, filling you with grace and peace.

"*How far that little candle
throws its beams!*"
WILLIAM SHAKESPEARE

OTHER CROWN CHAKRA ENERGIZING IDEAS The

Crown Chakra is associated with the pineal gland, which governs sleep and sleep patterns. Sleep is a big issue in today's world; many people feel they are not getting enough, or that the sleep they get is too light or disturbed. Good quality rest is vital to all body functions, repairing and restoring body and mind; during illness, it is often the best way to recover.

Free your sleep from technology

Finding ways to improve a daily pre-sleep routine is important, and this will benefit the energy of the Crown Chakra as well. Start right away by looking at your habits around electronic devices. For example, do you carry your mobile phone to bed with you, making it the last thing you see at night after being glued to it all day? Is there a TV in your bedroom as well? Do you spend a lot of time on a computer or a tablet during the day? If all these things are true and you find you can't get to sleep, or your sleep quality is poor, maybe it's time to re-examine these habits. Making sure there are no electronic devices in your sleeping space is very important. During the day,

artificial electromagnetic interference, radio waves and microwaves surround you all the time, everywhere you go; try and give your system a break from this when you settle down to sleep.

Changing your bedtime ritual

Try creating a different pre-sleep ritual for yourself. Switch off your devices. Take time to work on the Crown Chakra yoga and meditation exercises, or use the Crown Chakra tools on the following pages to help you. Go into your sleep mode with your mind in a clearer, more peaceful place. Rest well, to be ready for the new day.

CROWN CHAKRA ENERGY TOOLS

On these pages we will look at two crystals and an essential oil to use as energy tools to support and restore the energy of the Crown Chakra. As we saw at the beginning of this section, there are two colours to represent the Crown Chakra: white or purple.

Clear quartz crystal

The white or diamond brightness of the Crown Chakra can be energized and restored using clear quartz crystals. These can be found in points, clusters or large formations or as small polished tumblestones; choose a shape or form that appeals to you. Clear quartz is used in crystal healing to encourage energy to flow through all the chakras, especially the Crown Chakra.

Amethyst crystal

Amethyst is purple quartz; it can be found in pale lilac, purple and deep violet colours. Like clear quartz, it occurs in points, clusters, large pieces and small polished tumblestones. The purple energy of amethyst is very soothing to the brain, helping to calm anxiety. Putting an amethyst crystal under your pillow helps to support the Crown Chakra while you sleep. Amethyst is also very popular in jewellery; wear it to support your Crown Chakra during the day.

Lavender essential oil

Lavender is probably the most well-known essential oil, extracted from purple lavender flowers. It is so commonly used that its energetic qualities are often overlooked, but its soft, floral and fresh aroma relaxes the mind and soothes the spirits. Coming from purple flowers, this energy calms and restores the Crown Chakra. Putting two drops of lavender on your pillow can help you get a restful night's sleep. Adding four drops of lavender to an essential oil burner or a tissue on the windowsill spreads the gentle aroma into a room, creating a calm and relaxing space.

KEY CROWN CHAKRA ENERGY TOOLS

LAVENDER OIL	AMETHYST	INNER PEACE

ADDITIONAL CHAKRAS & ENHANCED ENERGY LEVELS

Within the field of holistic healing, in recent years there has been an expansion of the concept of the seven chakras to include five additional chakras and energy levels, making a total system of twelve. These 'new chakras' often feature in healing practice, for example spiritual or crystal healing. They are an advanced level of the chakras; before extending your practice into working with them, first it is important to work on balancing and restoring the seven main chakras.

The Thymus Chakra

The Thymus Chakra sits above the breastbone, in the centre of the upper chest. It links to the thymus gland, which supports the healthy function of the immune system. It is sometimes called the 'High Heart', or 'Thymic' or 'Pectoral Centre' in spiritual healing. It is considered to be a chakra linked with opening to a more spiritual life, where love on higher levels can flow into you and be expressed to the world. Sitting between the Heart and the Throat Chakras, when the Thymus Chakra is active, your spoken words come from a higher soul perspective with compassion, gentleness and kindness.

The colour of the Thymus Chakra is a soft turquoise, a blend of green and blue tones from the Heart and Throat Chakras. Being beside a turquoise or aquamarine-coloured sea is very beneficial to restore the energy of the Thymus Chakra.

Turquoise crystals

In crystal healing, stones like turquoise, aquamarine or labradorite, all of which have blue-green hues, are often placed on the location of the Thymus Chakra during a healing layout. This is when a person lies down on their back, and crystals are placed around them to create an individual healing matrix.

Atlas cedarwood

In aromatherapy, Atlas cedarwood essential oil helps to support and restore the energy of the Thymus Chakra. The warm, resiny and soothing aroma expands the chest and deepens breathing. It is also a good aid to meditation, with a calming effect on mind and heart; try adding four drops to an essential oil burner or onto a tissue on the windowsill.

CEDRVS foliis rigidis acutis perennantibus, conis subrotundis er

The Alta Major or Occipital Chakra

The Alta Major Chakra sits at the back of the cranium, right under the skull where the head and neck meet. If you feel the spot with your fingers, there is a slight indentation there; you can feel it when you move your head up and down. The Alta Major Chakra is connected to the occipital area at the back of the brain. It links to the Throat and Third Eye Chakras, once again as a means of higher energy expression. Sometimes the Alta Major Chakra is referred to as a place of dreaming, where visions and intuitive information from the Third Eye Chakra can be expanded, and then communicated via the Throat Chakra. This is a chakra with a deeply psychic effect, best explored with a teacher as a guide.

The colour of the Alta Major Chakra is usually considered to be magenta, a deep reddish-purple colour. It is an expression of the deep red of the Root Chakra travelling up the spine and combining with the purple of the Crown Chakra: a meeting between earth and heaven.

Rainbow moonstone

The Alta Major Chakra can be energized by wearing rainbow moonstone, a beautiful iridescent crystal which shines in mystical rainbow colours depending on the light. Rainbow moonstone can also be placed into a crystal healing layout for the same purpose.

Jasmine essential oil

In aromatherapy, the rich, warm and heady aroma of jasmine is a beautiful support to the Alta Major Chakra. It is expensive, but can be sourced already diluted in jojoba oil ready to apply to the skin. A few drops of jasmine in jojoba placed on the location of the Alta Major Chakra at the back of the head can be deeply soothing and supportive.

JASMINUM officinale.   JASMIN officinal.   *page 95*

The Earth Star Chakra

The Earth Star Chakra, sometimes called the Super Earth Chakra, is considered to be about eighteen inches below your feet, within the earth. This chakra sits beyond the structure of the physical body. When activated, it is your individual connection to the deep heart of the Earth, to the core of the living planet that supports us. It links to the Root Chakra at the base of the spine and enhances its grounding energy.

The colour of the Earth Star Chakra is a deep dark brown, a reflection of the many minerals, metals and organic constituents of the layers of the Earth. It has a warming and strengthening energy. The best way to meditate upon it is to actually stand barefoot on the Earth, and develop awareness of a ball of tingling energy right underneath your feet; however, you can practise this exercise indoors as well. Regular focused contact with the Earth keeps the Earth Star Chakra activated. It is a strong psychic protector.

Dark crystals

Protective crystals like black tourmaline or obsidian (which is actually volcanic glass from deep within the Earth) are excellent to wear or carry or use in crystal healing layouts to energize and restore the Earth Star Chakra.

Vetiver essential oil

In aromatherapy, vetiver essential oil is an excellent choice to support the Earth Star Chakra. The oil has a deep, smoky and earthy aroma; it is a thicker consistency than most essential oils and has a deep brown colour. On pages 144–149 you will find out more about essential oils and how to make a blend to use on your skin; a vetiver blend can be applied to the soles of your feet to help build a connection to the Earth Star Chakra.

Ramácciam.lu

The Soul Star & Stellar Gateway Chakras

The Soul Star and Stellar Gateway Chakras are beyond the physical body; they are usually represented in diagrams as sitting just above the head (Soul Star) and higher above the head (Stellar Gateway). Both of these chakras are extensions to the Crown Chakra, expanding into even higher levels of consciousness and spiritual experience.

We have already seen that the Crown Chakra represents a link to whatever you understand as source, spirit or God. This is already a level of awareness that can take a lifetime to experience. The Soul Star and Stellar Gateway Chakras take that awareness even further into cosmic realms of energy. Opening and working with these chakras takes many years of devoted spiritual practice. Attempting to work with such high energy frequencies on your own is not advised; a meditation or healing teacher is strongly recommended.

The higher realms

The Soul Star is a link to your soul, the level of your energy that has never left the Source; it stays with you during your life and returns to the Source when you pass on. In that way, we are all eternal beings.

The Stellar Gateway is the doorway to the universe itself, the vast spaces of stellar energy and dimensions beyond the conscious mind.

Pure light

These two chakras symbolize higher levels of light, so they are beyond the seven colour spectrum. In crystal healing, special transparent stones such as Herkimer diamonds, danburite or unusual forms of quartz such as Lemurian seed crystals may be used in layouts to symbolize these very high chakra energies.

Neroli oil

Essential oil of neroli (orange flower) has a subtle and unique energy vibration, gently supportive to the Crown Chakra and to both these higher chakras as well. Anointing the forehead with a neroli blend (see pages 144–149) helps to keep the Crown Chakra open and receptive to the potential of these higher energy frequencies.

WORKING WITH YOUR CHAKRAS

In this section you will find out how to start working with the energies in your chakras, how to decide which chakras need help, and which different tools to use. It is useful to read this whole section before you begin your chakra exploration, because you will probably find that certain tools appeal to you more than others. Always follow what feels right to you.

The Colour Energy Circuit

Now that we have examined the seven main chakras individually, it is important to sense all the chakras working together as levels in a whole system. This meditation will guide you into perceiving all the different chakra energies you have learned about as the colours of the spectrum, radiating throughout your energy field.

Sit comfortably on a firm-backed chair, feet uncrossed and flat on the floor, hands relaxed in your lap, or cross-legged on the floor if you prefer. You may wish to record this exercise to listen to.

Take a few deep breaths, relax, and let your mind be at peace.

Take your awareness into your Root Chakra at the base of your spine, with a deep red colour. Sense its warm energy spreading through the base of your spine and hips.

Now be aware of your Sacral Chakra, just below your navel, with its warm orange colour, spreading around your lower abdomen and lower back.

Now be aware of your Solar Plexus Chakra just under your ribs; sense the bright golden solar energy around your upper abdomen and middle back.

Move your awareness to your Heart Chakra in the centre of your chest; sense its rich green colour around your chest and shoulders.

Now be aware of your Throat Chakra at the base of your throat; sense its gentle blue colour, cool and soothing at the base of your neck.

Move your awareness up to your Third Eye Chakra between your eyebrows; sense its deep indigo colour, like the night sky.

Finally, be aware of the Crown Chakra at the top of your head, either as a white light or a rich purple colour, as you prefer.

Sit for a few moments, aware of these radiating colours. Then, starting at the Crown Chakra, see the colour diminish gently to a point, and close. Do this all the way down the spine for each chakra level. It is always important to close the levels after an exercise, to keep your system contained and balanced.

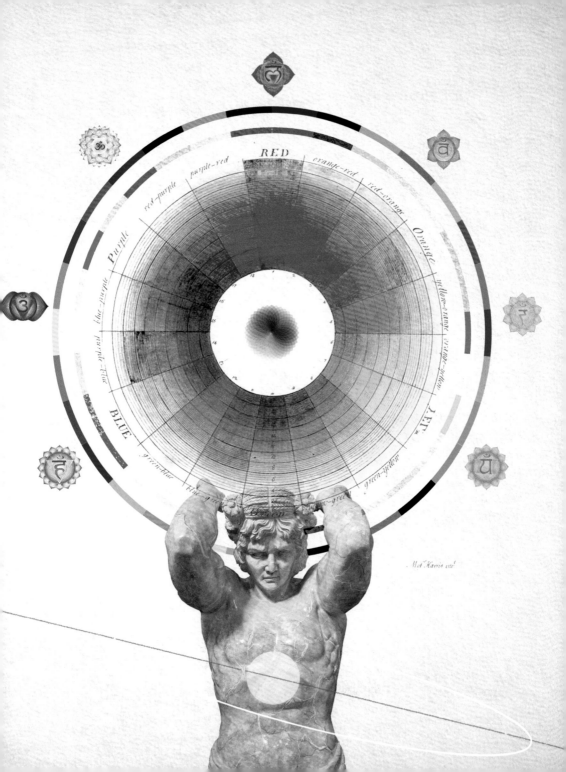

Yoga Sequence
for All Seven Chakras

Just as we had a yoga position in each chakra section, we can now join all of these poses together to make a yoga sequence to strengthen and nourish the whole chakra system. First, it is important to focus on learning each position individually to make sure you are doing it right; then practise them as a sequence. The sequence of seven positions bends and flexes the spine in different ways; during each pose, use your breathing to focus on the chakra that is being energized.

It will take about twenty minutes to complete a sequence. Start by lying down flat on the floor for few minutes, using your

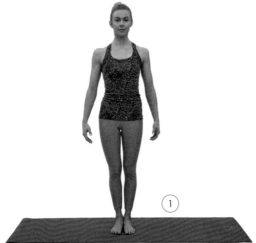

ROOT CHAKRA
Mountain Pose

SACRAL CHAKRA
Butterfly Pose

THROAT CHAKRA
Fish Pose

THIRD EYE CHAKRA
Downward Facing Dog Pose

breathing to relax and release the tension of the day. Then spend about two minutes going into, holding and coming out of each pose, and then at the end relax in Child's Pose for at least five minutes, or lie down comfortably stretched out on your back.

Regular practice of this routine will support and restore all your chakras as a whole system. Of course you can spend more time on positions that will help particular chakras that you feel need more energy.

When you feel ready, going to a yoga class with a qualified teacher is the best way to expand your yoga practice even further. There you will learn many more positions and sequences to restore and replenish your body, mind and spirit.

SOLAR PLEXUS CHAKRA
Camel Pose

HEART CHAKRA
Sphinx Pose

CROWN CHAKRA
Seated Forward Bend Pose

REST
Child's Pose

Seven Chakra Self-Healing Sequence

This exercise is a simple self-healing sequence where you place your hands over your chakra centres. It is very beneficial to practise this sequence as you relax in bed before sleep, as it calms your mind and helps you release the tensions and distractions of the day. You may even find you fall asleep before you have finished it, which is fine; it is a lovely way to drift gently into a peaceful slumber.

1 *Lie on your back comfortably in bed, covered up so you are warm and relaxed, your arms on top of the covers.*

2 *Place your hands on top of the cover, at the level of the Root Chakra. Let them rest gently there for a few moments. Breathe gently, and imagine rich red energy radiating from your hands into the area.*

3 *Move your hands to the level of your navel, the Sacral Chakra. As they rest there, imagine warm orange energy radiating from your hands into the area.*

4 *Now move your hands to the Solar Plexus Chakra between your ribs; imagine golden energy flowing from your hands into the area.*

5 *Move your hands to your Heart Chakra in the centre of your chest; feel vibrant green energy radiating from your hands into the area.*

6 *Now place your hands gently at the Throat Chakra; sense cool soft blue energy flowing into the area.*

7 *Using your left hand, place your fingers gently at your Third Eye Chakra; sense deep indigo energy bathing the area.*

8 *Now place both hands on top of your head, at your Crown Chakra; imagine purple or white light flowing into the area.*

9 *Bring your hands back down to your sides and breathe gently, feeling that all your energy centres are restored and balanced, your body is relaxed, your mind and heart at peace. Now you are ready for sleep.*

Giving & Receiving: Energy Flowing Through the Chakras

You may have noticed as we journeyed through the seven chakras individually that occasionally we referred to a chakra's energy being linked to receiving or giving. These two qualities add another layer of meaning to the chakras and to their effects on everyday life. The idea of yin and yang is another way of expressing this effect, yin being an inner state of receiving energy, and yang a way of giving or expressing energy outwards.

This table shows the seven chakras and their effects.

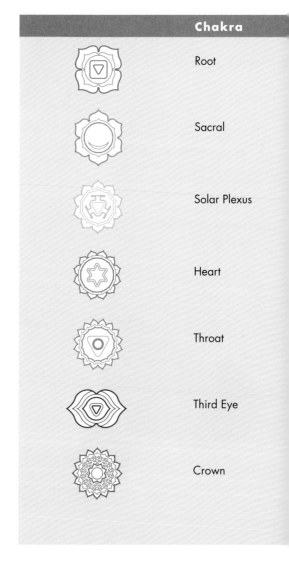

	Chakra
	Root
	Sacral
	Solar Plexus
	Heart
	Throat
	Third Eye
	Crown

Energy Quality	Effect
Giving Yang	The Root Chakra is where physical creative energy expresses itself outwards, for example, in the act of actually giving birth.
Receiving Yin	Sacral energy is linked to emotion and feelings and sexuality, and how we receive these energies from others.
Giving Yang	Solar Plexus energy is the personal power centre, linked to our outward actions in the world.
Receiving Yin	Heart Chakra energy is an inner state of receiving or radiating love and compassion from or to a person or one's family or on a wider level, for the world.
Giving Yang	Often a place of conflict, the Throat Chakra is where we literally express ourselves out to the world through our voice.
Receiving Yin	The intuitive Third Eye Chakra receives inspiration and creative flashes to spark changes in perception.
Balance Giving and Receiving	The Crown Chakra is a place where these two energies combine; we receive universal energy and we radiate that energy to the world.

Painting or Drawing Your Chakras

Now that you have learned more about all seven major chakras individually, an interesting thing to do is to explore for yourself what these energies mean to you. This exercise is designed to let your imagination and your intuitive mind loose onto paper to see what you create. It does not require you to be a painter or an artist, or to worry if you 'can draw'; it is a lovely excuse to let your mind play with the colours and express whatever you want. Just have fun!

You will need seven large sheets of plain paper and a set of watercolour or poster paints, or, if you like, you can use large felt-tip pens in the seven chakra colours. Each sheet of paper is for a separate chakra.

Let the spirit move you

Take a look at the seven colours and start just where you like; there is no need to follow a particular order. Use a felt-tip pen or paint in that chakra colour, place it on the page, and see where you go. You might start painting or drawing shapes, or just filling in an area with the colour to really sense it. You might draw objects or symbols that feel right to you in that colour. If you want to add shades of that colour, lighter and darker, that is fine, but try to stick to just one colour on the page.

Take your time

This exercise might take you a little while: you might do it over several days, or maybe in a burst of creativity, you might find yourself doing all of it in one day. When you have completed all seven sheets, lay them out on the floor and look at them together. This is your very own expression of the energy in your chakras. If you found it easier to work in some shades rather than others, just note this: the colours where you found it a challenge show you those chakras need some energy.

Which Chakras Need Help? Getting Started

As we saw on the previous page, working with the colours through paint or drawing can highlight chakras where you feel less of a connection with the energy; this is a sign that those chakras need some help. Here are some other suggestions on how to identify and start working to support your own chakra energy system.

Repeat the meditation exercise on pages 128–129, in which you visualize each colour band at the level of each chakra on the body. This time as you do the exercise, be aware of how intensively you can visualize and sense each energy level. It is quite normal to feel some levels more strongly than others; those that feel less intense or even weak are those that need some support.

If a few levels show up as weak, then sit quietly and ask yourself: which one needs energy first? Follow your intuition. Then, when you have your answer, go back to the section on that chakra and read it through again carefully. Set aside some time to think about the chakra quote, do the chakra yoga pose and sit in meditation, also using the energy tools for that chakra to support your practice.

After you have done some restoration work, have another look at the image you produced for that chakra. Can you see how to make that image come alive? What does your intuition tell you now?

Be gentle with yourself: don't rush this process. It is your personal experience. Once you feel that you have better energy in a chakra, notice how that makes you feel overall. Repeat the energy band visualization again and see how the levels feel now. You may find that the whole picture has already shifted. Energizing one chakra will affect all the others; you may find that your next chakra to work on is not what you expected. This is the magic of the journey.

Dowsing the Chakras

Dowsing is using a pendulum, a weight on the end of a cord or chain to obtain 'yes' or 'no' answers. If the pendulum is managed correctly, the answers come more from instinct than from logic; it is a way of bypassing what you think answers should be. Dowsing is another way to check the chakras and find out whether they need support.

Dowsing does not suit everyone; if you are a very analytical person, it may be a bit of a challenge for you to 'let the pendulum work'. Some people have a knack for dowsing, others not.

Making your pendulum

You can use lots of things as a pendulum, for example a crystal pendant on a thong, a chain with a medallion on it, or threading a piece of string through a pebble with a hole in it. The main thing is, you need a small weight on the cord or chain.

The dowsing process

Wrap the cord or chain around your first finger so the pendulum is few inches long. Hold it so the weight is still. Then ask, either in your mind or aloud, 'Show me "yes"'. The pendulum usually starts to move, often in a clockwise direction. Let it be still again. Then ask, 'Show me "no"'. Here the pendulum often moves from side to side. Once you try your yes and no reponses a few times, test it with your name: first, 'My name is…' [your true name], then a name that is not yours. If the responses are correct, you have a working pendulum.

Then, holding the pendulum in your right hand, touch each of your chakra points with your left hand, each time asking 'Does this chakra need energy?' See what the pendulum shows. As you practice, you may find the pendulum spins with different intensity: for example you might get a faint 'no', or a much stronger 'no'. Strong responses are the ones to notice; use this information to guide you into your chakra work.

Using Aromatherapy to Balance the Chakras

Aromatherapy is the use of pure essential oils, which are aromas extracted from flowers, herbs, fruit, leaves, wood or roots, to improve health and wellbeing. These pure scents of nature soothe the mind, uplift the emotions and also ease physical tension in the body. They are ideal tools to help balance and restore the chakras. Essential oils can be used in a number of ways.

Applied to the skin already diluted in jojoba oil

This applies to extremely precious and expensive floral essential oils like rose, jasmine and neroli (orange blossom). Since these oils are sold already diluted, this means they can be used directly on the skin as natural perfumes, and are also more affordable. (See resources section for list of suggested suppliers.)

Applied to the skin by making a blend

To make a simple blend, measure 20 ml or 4 teaspoons of vegetable oil, such as sunflower, sweet almond or grapeseed, into a small bottle. Add 4 drops of one essential oil to make a 1% dilution, safe for application to all skin types including sensitive. Close the bottle and shake it. Your blend is ready to use.

Vaporized into a room via a fragrance burner or diffuser

4–6 drops of essential oil used in a fragrance burner or a diffuser gives about an hour of aroma.

Vaporized into a room using a tissue

Add 4 to 6 drops of an essential oil to a tissue, and leave it on a windowsill or a radiator. This is not as effective as using a burner or diffuser but still gives an experience of the aroma.

Caution

Essential oils are highly concentrated with powerful aromas. Using essential oils is very beneficial; however, a few safety guidelines are necessary:

1 Never swallow essential oils.

2 Never use essential oils neat on the skin. Always blend an essential oil in a base oil (see opposite) before applying it to the skin.

3 If you are pregnant or think you may be, only use essential oils in the vaporizer. Application to the skin should not be done except by a qualified therapist.

ESSENTIAL OILS FOR HEALING THE CHAKRAS

In chapter 2, where each chakra was explored individually, each chakra was given an essential oil as a special energy tool. Essential oils are delicate energetic substances and they resonate very well with the subtle energies of the chakra system. In Ayurveda, the ancient Indian system of traditional medicine, applying essential oils to the chakras and other associated points on the body is an important aspect of healing body, mind and spirit.

The Essential Oils Selected for the Seven Chakras

BENZOIN

SANDALWOOD

LEMON

ROSE IN JOJOBA

Root Chakra
Apply to the base
of the spine.

Sacral Chakra
Apply to just below
the navel.

Solar Chakra
Apply to
just under the ribs.

Heart Chakra
Apply in the middle
of the chest.

The essential oil suggestions on this page are a starting point; many other essential oils can be blended to work with the chakras. However, from this list you can always make a simple blend which can add an extra dimension to your work with a particular chakra.

To apply your blend, tip your bottle to coat your fingertips with a little oil – you do not need much – and apply it gently to your skin at the level of the chakra you are working on. Use a clockwise circular motion on an area about the size of your palm.

Blend Proportions

To make a blend, select one essential oil for the chakra you are working on, add 4 drops into 20 ml or 4 teaspoons carrier oil in a small bottle, shake the mixture and the blend is ready.

ROMAN
CHAMOMILE

Throat Chakra
Apply to the base
of the throat.

FRANKINCENSE

Third Eye Chakra
Apply between the eyebrows. Avoid
the inner eye area; essential oils can
sting if they get into the eyes.

LAVENDER

Crown Chakra
Apply on the top
of your head.

If you are working with a particular chakra over a few days, you can apply your blend to that chakra each time you do your healing practice.

ADVANCED AROMATHERAPY CHAKRA BLENDS If you

are already interested or qualified in aromatherapy and you have a wider collection of
essential oils, you may wish to make more advanced blends to restore and heal different
chakras. These blends use combinations of three essential oils to complement the
energy of the seven chakras. The resulting aromas are more complex and interesting;
they are especially enhancing and reviving to the energy levels of the chakras.

These blends are diluted at the stronger
level of 2.5% (10 drops in 20 ml or
4 teaspoons base oil). This dilution is
suitable for normal skin. If your skin
is sensitive, halve the number of drops to
add to the base oil.

Notice that the central column shows the
original essential oils chosen for the seven
chakras, with the additional essential oils
on either side, balancing them to make
the blends.

Choose a blend for a chakra you are
working on, and apply it as directed on
pages 144–145.

Chakra	Essential Oil 1	Essential Oil 2	Essential Oil 3	Blend Effect
Root	Vetiver, 2 drops	Benzoin, 4 drops	Ginger, 4 drops	Energizing, with a warm, spicy, sweet aroma
Sacral	Jasmine in jojoba, 4 drops	Sandalwood, 2 drops	Sweet orange, 4 drops	Energizing, with an exotic, woody floral aroma
Solar Plexus	Atlas cedarwood, 4 drops	Lemon, 4 drops	Eucalyptus, 2 drops	Expansive and opening, with a woody, fresh aroma
Heart	Grapefruit, 4 drops	Rose in jojoba, 4 drops	Petitgrain (orange leaf), 2 drops	Soothing, with a soft, floral citrus aroma
Throat	Bergamot, 2 drops	Roman chamomile, 4 drops	Lemon eucalyptus, 4 drops	Soothing, with a light citrus, fresh and sweet aroma
Third Eye	Myrtle, 4 drops	Frankincense, 4 drops	Mandarin, 2 drops	Expansive, with a spicy, fresh and euphoric aroma
Crown	Neroli in jojoba, 4 drops	Lavender, 4 drops	Geranium, 2 drops	Gentle and calming with a soft floral aroma

Back Massage
with Chakra Healing

This simple back routine works well if you have a friend or a partner who can give you a massage, or if you want to give a massage to someone who needs some healing energy. The person receiving needs to lies down on their front, on the floor on a comfortable pad, and the massager kneels beside them on their right side to work. They need to undress the top half of the body; cover their legs with a blanket to keep them warm. Select a blend to work on a particular chakra as appropriate to your chakra healing practice.

1 *Kneel by the person's right side at the level of their waist and hips. Pour a teaspoon of the blend into your hands and place them on either side of the spine, on the lower back. Stroke up the sides of the spine, out over the shoulders and down the sides of the back; repeat this movement three times.*

2 *Place your right hand on their right shoulder, and your left hand on their left hip. Stroke down the body with your right hand and up with your left hand, at the same time; this is a warming alternate movement to the sides of the body. Repeat four times.*

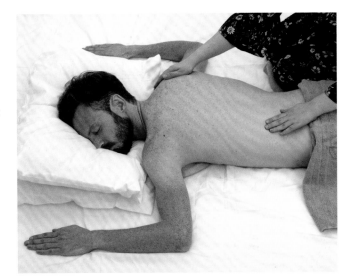

3 *Place your hands back on either side of the spine. Fan your hands out to the side of the body, pressing outwards. Do this slowly at the lower back, mid back, upper back and over the shoulders. Repeat this sequence twice.*

151

4 Now, bearing in mind the particular chakra the person is working on, kneel facing across the body and place your hands over that particular chakra area. Feel the energy of the blend under your hands, and sense it working its way into that chakra, giving it energy. Hold this position for about a minute.

5 *Finally, stroke gently down the sides of the body, cover the person with a big towel and a blanket and let them rest and absorb the energy of the blend.*

Crystals & Chakra Healing

In Chapter 2, as we explored each chakra individually, a crystal was assigned to each one as a special healing tool. Crystals are beautiful gifts from the Earth in many colours and shapes; they have fascinated human beings for thousands of years. In crystal healing, they are used in different ways to balance, restore and energize the chakras.

The crystals recommended here are all available as small loose stones, which is all you need to begin with. After you have bought them, clean them by running them under cold water, dry them with a soft cloth and then keep them together in a drawstring bag.

Crystal suppliers sell these and many other crystals in larger pieces, some polished, some not, in a whole range of sizes. You may very well start adding to your collection; your intuition will guide you to choose crystals that feel right to you.

CROWN
amethyst or clear
quartz

THIRD EYE
lapis lazuli

THROAT
blue lace agate

HEART
rose quartz (pink for
unconditional love) or
aventurine (green for
expansive growth)

SOLAR PLEXUS
citrine

SACRAL
amber

ROOT
red jasper

SIMPLE CRYSTAL HEALING METHODS

The crystals on the previous pages correspond to the chakras by their colours, which makes it easy to select the ones you need. You can use your crystals in different ways; here are a few suggestions to help you.

Meditate with a crystal

When you first buy a crystal, sit quietly holding it in your cupped hands, close your eyes and focus on it. As you sit, you may notice your hands begin to tingle, or feel sensations in other parts of your body. Speak this intention: 'This crystal is a pure reflection of light and love.'

After this, use the crystal as it is needed in your chakra work, and hold it as you sit in meditation for that particular chakra, to amplify its energy.

Bathe with a crystal

As you work with a particular chakra, for example the Heart Chakra, try placing your rose quartz crystal in the bath with you. Crystals transmit their energy easily into water; this way, your bath becomes a healing treatment.

Sleep with a crystal

Gentle crystals like rose quartz or amethyst help to soothe the mind and improve sleep; try placing a small crystal under your pillow for a peaceful night's rest.

Hold a crystal to a chakra

When you work on a particular chakra, try lying down comfortably, holding the crystal linked to that chakra on the body location; this energizes and supports it. If you are working on the Crown Chakra, you will need to place the crystal on the pillow above your head.

Place a crystal on every chakra

This is a simple crystal healing layout which is best done with a friend's help. Lie down comfortably on the floor; your friend needs to place the crystals on your body in the order of the chakras and their colour. The Root Chakra stone can be placed between the legs and the Crown Chakra stone above the head. Then you rest in the energy matrix created by all the stones working together with all your chakras.

CRYSTALS & CHAKRAS IN DAILY LIFE

The beauty of crystals is that they can be carried with you every day, so you can take the supportive energy of chakra healing into the world. As you travel, work, shop, exercise at the gym, spend time with your friends and family, chakra energy will go with you. This is a way to feel more confident and empowered in your daily life. Try these suggestions to get started.

Wearing chakra-themed jewellery

Choosing to wear a crystal that corresponds to a chakra is more than simply wearing a piece of jewellery; it means that you carry that energy with you during your day. You may choose to wear a crystal linked to the chakra you are working on at the time, or one that suits a particular situation. For example, if you are going into a big meeting and you need to speak your mind, you could choose a blue crystal like blue moonstone to support your Throat Chakra, or a yellow crystal like citrine to support your Solar Plexus Chakra if you feel nervous.

Carrying a crystal

If you don't want to show the chakra you are working on, then simply carry your chosen chakra crystal with you in a small drawstring bag. This can be slipped into a pocket or a handbag. If you feel nervous about travelling or you are stressed at work, smoky quartz is a very good protective crystal to carry to neutralize negative energy.

Chakra support in a new environment

This is a particularly useful technique when you are away from home. Take your bag of chakra crystals with you and a small silk scarf in a colour that you like. When you get to your hotel room, lay your scarf on a table and place your chakra crystals in a circle. Sit quietly and pick up each stone in turn for a few moments, tuning into the energy of the chakra that goes with it. By the end of the exercise your energy will be more grounded in the new environment. This is also helpful for jet-lag.

Colour Healing

Colour healing is a special kind of holistic healing where therapists channel different coloured energy through their hands placed on different parts of the body. This kind of healing is very beneficial to receive, and leaves a person feeling deeply peaceful and rested. Sometimes colour healing is called 'spiritual healing'; this does not mean it is religious, it is simply healing coming from energy. On pages 132–135 there is a meditation where you place your hands on your chakra locations and visualize the colours; this is a form of colour healing.

As you become more used to the energies of the different chakras and are able to sense the colours, you may feel that you want to offer colour healing to someone else. If you do this, you need to be aware that the energy does not come from you, but flows through you; you are a channel for the energy to be shared.

Offering colour healing

Your friend needs to lie comfortably on their front, their arms and head supported on a pillow. You need to kneel by their side. Both of you take a few deep breaths.

1 *Cup your hands over the base of their spine. Breathe deeply, and sense the red energy of the Root Chakra.*

2 *Then move your hands up over their sacral bone, and sense the orange energy of the Sacral Chakra.*

3 *Move up to the mid back for the Solar Plexus Chakra and its gold energy.*

4 *Next, move up to the upper back for the green Heart Chakra energy.*

5 *Gently place your hands at the base of their neck for the blue Throat Chakra energy.*

6 *Move to the back of their head for the Third Eye indigo energy.*

7 *Finally place your hands on the top of their head for the white or purple Crown Chakra energy, as your intuition guides you. To finish, run your hands gently down their back from the shoulders to the hips, three times. After a few moments, you and your friend can share how this experience felt.*

COLOUR HEALING THROUGH FOOD

We have already talked about many different ways to experience energy through the chakras using different healing tools and approaches. Another vital way that we take energy into the body is through our food. As you become more conscious of chakra energy in your life, activated through the different colours in the spectrum, it makes sense to think about food as a way of adding another dimension to your energy work.

When we eat, different senses are activated. The smell of food makes our mouths water and our bodies get ready to digest; we touch different textures as we eat food. The sight of food, meanwhile, is as important as the taste or the aroma of it. Some culinary traditions like Japanese sushi, for example, make a play of different colours and shapes placed carefully on a plate.

How aware are you of colours as you put food onto a plate? How about doing that with more awareness? Arranging a salad, for example: rich green leaves, bright red tomatoes, warm orange grated carrot, pale green cucumber, bright yellow pepper . . . you can make a salad into a chakra energy treat.

Warming yourself up

If your energy is low, there is nothing like a warm vibrant curry full of rich spices to entice your appetite, and the warm colours energize your Root and Sacral Chakras. You could also try the spicy red of a Mexican chilli to get your Root Chakra energy going.

Colourful treats

Making smoothies is a great way to support the chakras too. Rich red berries for the Root Chakra, blue berries for the Throat and Third Eye Chakras, golden fruit like pineapple or mango for the Sacral or Solar Plexus Chakra: the creative possibilities are fun and endless.

Let your food be for your spirit and energy as well as for your body.

WEARING CHAKRA COLOURS

Choosing clothes to wear with chakra colours in mind is another way to carry that energy with you during your day. This works for both women and men: even in the office, a formal suit can be livened up with a colourful tie. If you have to wear a uniform to work, choose to wear your favourite chakra colours whenever you have time off.

Colour your world

Thinking about chakra colours when you choose clothes to wear brings a new zest to your everyday life – you can literally carry that energy into your day.

The main chakra colours are vivid shades of red, orange, yellow, green, blue, indigo and violet: the shades that light splits into in the colour spectrum. These exact shades might feel too bright or intense to wear, so try variations within the colours to symbolize a particular chakra. For example, bright orange does not suit everyone, but soft apricot shades are easier to wear. Strong purple might feel a bit overwhelming, but lighter purple or lilac shades are in the same theme.

What your tastes teach you

An interesting exercise to do is to go and look at your wardrobe. What colours dominate it? What have you picked instinctively as your tones? If you have a lot of black, grey and white, your life could definitely use some colour. If you want to explore more colours that suit you, colour consultants can help you find the right palette. Clever accessorizing (for example, with scarves) can carry a little chakra colour energy into your day, even into the workplace.

Next time you go shopping

What about buying yourself a set of T-shirts in the seven chakra colours? (Or shades of them that you feel comfortable with.) As you work on a particular chakra, try wearing the colour of that chakra as well; see if it adds a dimension to your chakra healing practice.

Sound & the Chakras

In the Throat Chakra section on pages 86–87, we did an exercise using the different vowel sounds as a simple vocal exercise to experience the effects of these sounds within the Throat Chakra itself. Sound and toning are very important aspects of chakra work. In Hindu and Buddhist traditions, sounds combined into sacred words and phrases are called mantras; these are toned or chanted many times for a healing effect.

The simple vocal exercise we did is actually a chakra balancing exercise too; the vowel sounds can be linked to the first five chakras.

A   Root Chakra
E   Sacral Chakra
I   Solar plexus Chakra
O   Heart Chakra
U   Throat Chakra

A

E

So toning the five vowel sounds together is very beneficial to energize and heal these five chakras in preparation for work at the higher levels of the Third Eye and Crown Chakras.

The simple vowel sounds clear and cleanse the energy vibrations as a beginning; then for the two higher chakras, chanting mantras is the next step.

Inspiring voices

A beautiful mantra is the well-known 'Om Mani Padme Hum', which can be toned on one note, at a level comfortable to your voice. This ancient and beautiful mantra is an expression of the 'jewel in the lotus', the symbol of the Crown Chakra; it has many meanings, including oneness with the universe, rising above suffering, and a radiation of love to all beings.

Listening to Buddhist monks chanting this mantra is very powerful; it is healing, soothing, and also uplifting. This mantra is hundreds of years old and originated in the high mountains of Tibet. The fact that it has been chanted so many millions of times over so many years gives these sounds deep power and meaning. This mantra strengthens and replenishes all the chakras, especially the Third Eye and Crown Chakras.

I   O   U

ANCIENT INDIAN CHAKRA SOUNDS

In Hindu traditions, the seven major chakras each have their own sounds. These are called 'bijas', which means 'seed sounds'. These sounds are an ancient aspect of the chakra system, going back to its deepest roots. As seed sounds, they are single syllables, individual elements of consciousness, expressed through the voice at a particular resonance, leading to the highest level of spiritual vibration at the Crown Chakra.

Chanting the bijas is an expression of universal love. As you learn these syllables, try and concentrate on the relevant chakra at the same time; be aware of the resonance of these sounds in the locations of the centres. It is best to do this practice sitting cross-legged on the floor, or if that is not comfortable, sit up straight on a firm-backed chair and place your feet flat on the ground, your hands resting lightly in your lap.

Bijas

Notice that the two higher chakras are expressed as Om, the first syllable in 'Om mani padme hum'. Om is a very powerful syllable to chant; it calms the mind, soothes fraught emotions and brings a sense of inner peace and harmony.

As you chant the bijas, you are healing and energizing each chakra in turn with its own special and ancient vibration. Each of the first five syllables is made up of consonants surrounding the vowel sound in the middle; in ancient Hindu tradition, the vowel sounds are eternal spirit, and the consonants bring them to earth. The Om is a pure balance of one vowel, one consonant – earth and spirit in perfect harmony.

The Bijas

Root Chakra ~ *Lam*

Sacral Chakra ~ *Vam*

Solar Plexus Chakra ~ *Ram*

Heart Chakra ~ *Yam*

Throat Chakra ~ *Ham*

Third Eye Chakra ~ *Om*

Crown Chakra ~ *Om*

SOUND HEALING TOOLS Sound healing using particular tools is

an ancient practice with its roots in Tibet and China. The instruments shown on these pages resonate at particular notes which correspond to the energies of the chakras. Placing them on or around the body, or playing them close to the body, transmits the vibration of sound into the person's individual energetic field, helping to promote deep feelings of relaxation and peace. You will find that certain tones and sounds appeal to you and feel good when you listen to them – these are the ones you need.

Bowls

We saw on page 23 that Tibetan bowls, unique hand beaten metal bowls made of a traditional combination of precious metals, can be vibrated or even placed on the body to transmit the resonance of sound into the chakras.

The art of Tibetan bowls also tunes different sized bowls to energize different chakras. If you want to buy a bowl, check which chakra it is tuned to. When you like the sound of a bowl, it is resonating with you; it can be interesting to find out which chakra is responding, because it is asking for energy.

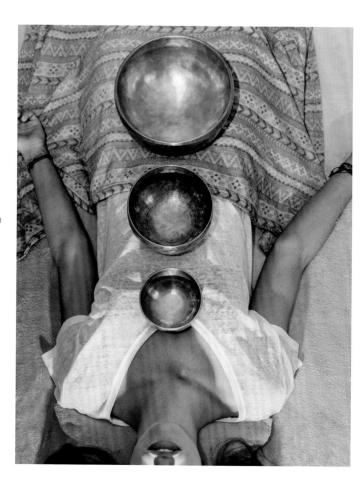

Gongs

Chinese metal gongs are a much larger extension of the bowls; these are still beaten into shape using time-honoured selections of different metals. Gongs can have many different sounds, some high and bright, resonating with the higher chakras, and some deep and resonant, energizing the lower chakras. Sound healers using gongs will position them at your head or at your feet, so the vibration of the sound passes over you like a wave. Huge gongs were used in the ancient Chinese royal court – their sound is like heavenly doors opening.

Chimes

In the Chinese art of feng shui, chimes are a simple and beautiful way to bring beneficial sound waves into your space. They are available made of metal, wood or bamboo; listen to them carefully and your intuition will guide you to the sound that feels good to you. Positioned outside in a garden, they give a gentle ripple of sound; inside, you can run a finger over them to cleanse your space with their soft tinkling notes.

A SOUND HEALING TREATMENT

The ultimate in sound healing treatment is a marvellous healing experience called a sound bath. Sound healers use many different sound tools: bells, chimes, gongs, Tibetan bowls and singing bowls carved from crystal, combining to create beautiful combinations of sounds and vibrations all around your body.

To experience a sound bath, you simply lie down in a relaxed state to receive the sounds and vibrations, which tune and energize all your chakras and bring your body and mind into balance. Having a sound bath calibrated to your healing needs is also a wonderfully relaxing experience. It is well worth finding out if there are any sound healers in your area so you can try this treatment.

Being your own healer

If no sound healer is available, it is worth exploring the realm of healing music, available on CD or via streaming services. Every culture has its own definition of healing sound: the pipes of the Andes, the chimes and bells of Tibet, the gongs of China, the shamanic drums and chants of Native American Indians, or the beautiful harmonies of Gregorian chant.

In New Age music there are many kinds of sound-healing CDs available, some carefully focused on chakra healing; investigate which ones appeal to you and let your intuition guide your choice.

Discovering your sound

Listening to your favourite kind of healing music is a very beneficial dimension to your chakra healing practice; try working with background music or in silence, and notice how both experiences are supportive in different ways.

Exploring different traditions of healing sound through music is a fascinating journey, especially as you find the particular sounds or styles that work for you. The more you work on your chakras, the more attuned your senses will be to the kind of vibrations that support and heal your system.

CHAKRA ENERGIES IN DAILY LIFE

This section explores how to observe the energies of the chakras as you go about your daily life. Now that you understand them better, you will begin to see how different chakra energies show up in other people's actions or in different life situations. This understanding is a marvellous tool for increasing self-awareness in life, helping you appreciate other people's energies as well as your own.

Observing the Chakras at Work: Introduction

Here we are going to explore how to observe the chakras in daily life, in the world we work in.

During our journey we have explored the chakras individually in detail and looked at ways to understand them, know them, experience them and restore them. As you work with your chakras and feel their energy improving, it can be tempting to keep this practice completely separate from daily life, to think of it as something 'spiritual' as opposed to 'everyday'. However, while it is good to maintain a special quiet space for spiritual practice, there is also a benefit in allowing this new awareness to permeate other aspects of your life.

How? Well, now that you know and understand the chakras and their energies better, you can begin to pick up signs, types of behaviour, activities you do, things you feel good at and things that challenge you in your daily life, and understand these through the template of the seven chakra energies.

Appreciating others

It's also likely that you will start to observe these signs in other people too. All of us have strengths and weaknesses, things we do well and things we find difficult. All of us have talents that make us shine, indicating strong chakra energies. We are all fascinating and different; understanding and observing the chakras as they manifest in other people can help you in your relationships and work, giving more clarity to your communication and interactions.

Crown Chakra People: Visionaries

Take a look around you. Every single object that you see – a book, a candle, a computer, a plate, a pen – had to be made by somebody somewhere at some time. In order for those objects to be made, somebody had to have the idea to do it. For a plate, it might have been the idea to make a plate with a particular shape or colour or pattern. For a book, it might have been a desire to write a story on a particular subject. For a computer, it might have been an idea to make a machine that is smaller but still very powerful. The point is, before any of these things become real, somebody has to think of doing it.

Ideas come from creativity, and creativity is the realm of the Crown Chakra. When the other chakras are balanced and open, this paves the way for the creative energy to flow in. Often there is a spark, a moment of thinking, 'That's it!' This is the trigger for the energy of the idea to take shape in the mind. At this stage, it does not matter how this idea is going to take physical shape in reality. All that matters is the inspiration, and letting it flow.

Appreciating the innovators

In any workplace there are 'visionaries' or 'ideas people'. You might be one yourself. These people are not practical, they might stumble when asked to do mundane tasks, but they excel at coming up with inspiration, and ideas are what push human life forward. These people are very connected to their Crown Chakra.

If you hear yourself criticizing someone, saying, 'He's always in his head!' then perhaps now you see that person has a gift to offer. We all have ideas, and they are to be treasured. Perhaps you do, and you feel that your ideas are not always heard. By nourishing your Crown Chakra and encouraging the spark of creative energy to flow through you, you will build your confidence to express your inspiration.

Third Eye Chakra People: Designers

Intuition is intriguing; some people call it a 'sixth sense'. It's an inner certainty that something works in a particular way, without knowing why; it's not logical, but somehow it's right. Intuition lets us make links between things, places, people or ideas in a lightning-quick way that can be surprising. The art of working with intuition is to learn to trust it.

People with strong intuitive skills can take the pure idea of the visionary and start to place it in a context, sensing how, where, why it will be useful or helpful. They are very connected to their Third Eye Chakra. In the workplace, a visionary has the spark of an idea, and an intuitive person will grasp it and start to shape it. They are designers. They might start a mind-map or draw a table or a sketch. Graphic designers work on this level: they take the idea for a product and make it visual, starting to give it shape, colour and identity. At this stage, the product itself does not yet exist, but the 'look' of it is already appearing.

Advertising and media work very much at this level too: the constant bombardment of images we receive during our day from internet-connected devices, billboards and TV is intense. All these images are intended to stimulate us to want the products that are being shown: we don't have the experience of them physically yet, but the images make links in our minds to make us want these things.

Keeping clear-sighted

In modern times it is very important to build and strengthen the energy of the Third Eye Chakra. The intensity of the media around us distracts us from using our own intuitive energy by substituting it with ideas from other sources. We forget to use our own intuition, and, like any skill, it gets rusty. The good news is, by doing Third Eye Chakra work, we can get our own intuition working again.

Throat Chakra People: Communicators

The Throat Chakra is all about speaking, singing, using the voice, and communication. This is the chakra level where visionary ideas and intuitive links start to be talked about, expressed verbally, shared with other people. When you see someone who is very relaxed and at ease sharing ideas, teaching, explaining things so other people can understand or giving speeches in front of a large audience, it's easy to think, 'Wow, that's a real talent.' It really means that person is very connected to their Throat Chakra; the energy is open and flowing, their words come out easily and they communicate successfully.

In the world of music, whatever the style, there may be lots of tunes around, but the ones that really last in your mind are sung by people with real talent, who can channel energy through the Throat Chakra and make sounds that touch you and spark your feelings. (If the song really strikes a chord with you, you are likely to feel it in your Heart Chakra; music works on many levels.)

Finding your voice

Some people have real talent at the Throat Chakra level and others struggle with it. Many feel they can't express their truth, for whatever reason: shyness, lack of personal confidence, a feeling that they are not good enough to speak. In the workplace, some people find that being asked to give a presentation is a cue for sleepless nights and sweating fear beforehand, and on the day their throat constricts with anxiety. If this sounds like you, then try practising the Throat Chakra exercises and carry energy tools with you into the situation; by raising and energizing the chakra, you can give that presentation with better confidence.

Heart Chakra People: Carers

There is a phrase: 'To put your heart into what you do.' This describes those who do what they do for love. We all know these kinds of people – they are carers.

Examples of human generosity are everywhere. Parents have to juggle so many aspects of modern life to care for their children. Nurses, doctors, midwives, paramedics, carers or therapists, are dedicated to looking after others, often coming into those professions because they feel a deep vocation, a motivation to help and support other people in times of need. Volunteers do unsung things for no financial gain, just from the motivation of helping to make people's lives better. There are many more examples. Putting your heart into what you do is an investment of a different kind; you are not doing it for the money, you are doing it for the greater good. This shows a strong Heart Chakra connection.

Preserving love

On a simple daily level, it may be that you are someone who cares about other people, that you like to support them and be there when they need you. You may be the person that others come to when they need a listening ear, a loving hug, a quiet time to express what is happening to them. You are expressing the energy of your Heart Chakra.

It is important for people with a strong Heart Chakra impulse to make sure that their own Heart Chakra is constantly re-energized and restored. Symptoms like exhaustion, stress, overload and burnout are signs that the Heart Chakra is totally depleted: the reserves are all 'given out'. You cannot continue to give on the Heart Chakra level if you are depleted. All the Heart Chakra exercises and tools are there to be used to help restore and re-energize the Heart centre. Being a Heart Chakra person actually means taking good care of yourself first so you have the energy to give to others.

Solar Plexus Chakra People: Leaders

People with a strong Solar Plexus Chakra are natural leaders who can direct others. They are strong-minded individuals who are comfortable with their own personal power. In a positive situation, leadership like this can be inspirational and encourage those who follow to work to their best individual potential. In the workplace, these might be managers, directors, supervisors – anyone with responsibility for a group of people. Taking this kind of leadership role is not for everyone, but in order for organizations, businesses and countries to thrive, confident leaders are necessary to get things moving.

The Solar Plexus Chakra is the place of personal power: remember, its Sanskrit name, Manipura, means 'place of the jewel', and its element is fire. It is a very powerful chakra where we manifest our will in the world.

Healthy power

If the power of will is projected with the intention to create a positive result, the Solar Plexus Chakra is serving its highest purpose. However, this chakra also has the potential to be pushed out of balance and become over-stimulated. If the sense of will and personal power is only for one's own good, or if it is used to suppress others or to get one's own way, this is the negative aspect of Solar Plexus Energy. Think about fire: if used benevolently, it brings a welcome brightness and warmth, but a fiery inferno can destroy.

Preserving balance

The Solar Plexus Chakra needs to be balanced with the energy of the Heart Chakra so the sense of will is balanced with the energy of unconditional love. Solar Plexus Chakra energy is vital to the system because it provides the flame, the energy to get things happening; we all need it to make progress in life. However, our personal will needs to work in harmony with the needs of those around us.

Sacral Chakra People: Networkers

Some people are naturally very sociable: they want to share with others and link people together. They are natural networkers; they have wide circles of friends; they believe that in order to move life along you need the right people to do it. Warm, open, friendly people with a welcoming manner, they have no problem arranging seating plans for a big dinner: they know exactly who should be sitting with whom. These people are very in touch with Sacral Chakra energy.

In the working world, Sacral Chakra people work through contacts: 'It's not what you know, it's who you know.' They are the ones who instantly know who to ring or email when something is needed, and understand the value of hospitality, including entertaining, to make good contacts to further business interests. Working in co-operation with others suits them better than working on their own, and they thrive in focus groups, meetings and brainstorming activities. Sharing work with others brings out the best in them.

Boosting your social energy

If you are uncomfortable being a 'sharer', or if you find groups of people overwhelming and you tend to choose to be on your own, it is likely that your Sacral Chakra is depleted and needs some help. Working on this chakra is not going to turn you into a people person overnight, but it may help you to feel more comfortable and open in social situations, and more aware of opportunities being offered to you to share activities and time with others.

Sacral Chakra energy is warm, open, joyful and spontaneous, all excellent qualities to have to build rich and rewarding friendships. No man is an island, as the saying goes: as human beings, we have developed as a species because we have learned to live, love and work together. Keeping the Sacral Chakra energized supports a truly social life.

Root Chakra People: Doers

When we talked about visionaries, ideas people, we said that these people are less comfortable doing physical tasks because they are working at the Crown Chakra level. However, none of their ideas could ever take physical shape without those who work at the opposite end of the spectrum: the doers. These are the people who roll up their sleeves, get stuck in and do what is needed to turn the idea into reality. They are Root Chakra people; practical, grounded, with hands-on skills, willing to sweat for a result if necessary. They are vital to the successful achievement of any creative idea.

If we take the example of creating a new building, the visionary needs to come up with the building's purpose, then an architect creates a design, but the building doesn't come into reality until somebody puts bricks and mortar together with practical skills to ensure that building will last. Doers are people with particular skills; they are just as vital as ideas people, but do not always get the respect they deserve.

Good sense in action

Doers will ask questions like, 'So how does that work in practice?', because they want to know the practical implications of something they are being asked to consider. These aspects are often overlooked by people who spend more time in the realm of ideas, so doers provide a vital balance.

If you consider yourself to be more of an ideas person, it can be an interesting personal challenge to do some Root Chakra work to stimulate that energy in your system and see what happens. You might suddenly be inspired to learn a new practical skill. In life, it is always possible to choose to do something different. Try it: you never know what it might open up.

Check Your Chakra Strengths & Challenges

Now that we have explored different aspects of the chakras manifesting in everyday life, try this exercise to check your own chakra talents and challenges. There is no good or bad, plus or minus here: it's just about learning how things are, and looking at areas you might be able to change if you want to.

Chakra exercise

A local group you are associated with wants to raise some money to refurbish a building that you use.

Now read the statements opposite. It is likely that at least one or two make you think, 'Yes, I would do this.' Also look at the ones where you think, 'No, this isn't me.' This little exercise shows the chakra energies that are more dominant in you, and those where you feel challenged. Now you know what to do if you want to change this situation, try some chakra work on those areas and see what happens! You now have the tools to make changes in your life.

Third Eye
I want to design a fund-raising web page to support the activity.

Sacral
I ring around and email all the people I know to get them to come to a meeting.

Heart
I feel that this idea is wonderful and I care about getting it right.

Throat
I am interviewed by the local paper and tell them all about the fund-raising.

Crown
I come up with a brilliant fundraising idea.

Solar Plexus
I chair a fundraising meeting and take the lead in bringing people together.

Root
I walk around the streets putting leaflets through people's doors.

CHAKRA ENERGIES AT HOME

In this section you will find out how to enhance different areas in your home with different chakra energies; this turns your living environment into a truly beneficial and healing personal space. As you practise raising your awareness of your chakras within, you can also extend new energy into your external environment, to create true balance in your life.

Root Chakra:
Home as a Sanctuary Space

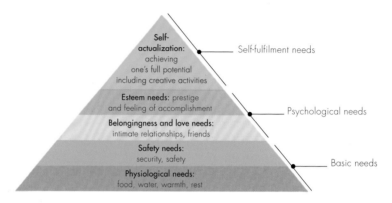

Self-actualization: achieving one's full potential including creative activities — Self-fulfilment needs

Esteem needs: prestige and feeling of accomplishment

Belongingness and love needs: intimate relationships, friends — Psychological needs

Safety needs: security, safety — Basic needs

Physiological needs: food, water, warmth, rest

The idea of home as a safe place is deeply rooted in human consciousness.

In the 1950s, a psychologist called Abraham Maslow created a model called the hierarchy of needs.

In some ways this diagram resembles our chakra chart: at the bottom are two levels linked to basic needs, then the middle levels are psychological needs, and the upper level is linked to self-fulfilment.

At the level of basic needs, security and safety, along with physical survival needs like food and shelter, are vital to human mental and physical wellbeing. Home is more than just four walls; it needs to reflect a deep sense of grounding and rooting and feeling secure in that place.

Your own place

How do you feel in your home? Does it feel like a safe place to come back to? We don't necessarily mean having locks on the doors and windows and a security alarm here, it's more about how your home is working as a sanctuary for you. This is linked to Root Chakra energy. Do you feel you belong in your home? How does the energy of your home suit you, inside and out? If you have chosen your home yourself, most likely it will suit you; however, if you have had to move somewhere that is not entirely your choice, you may feel less at ease.

Emotional home-making

Using an incense ceremony is a wonderful way to clear the space inside your home before adding some Root Chakra energy. Use a stick of your favourite incense or some sage leaves burned on a charcoal pellet in a small heatproof dish. As the incense burns, practise your Root Chakra meditation to feel very present and grounded in your space. Place a smoky quartz crystal in a central location in your space to protect you from any negative energies in your environment. By doing these things, you bring Root Chakra energy into your space to build yourself a personal sanctuary.

Sacral Chakra: Home as a Welcoming Space

The Spanish saying 'mi casa, su casa' ('my home is your home') illustrates very well how to bring Sacral Chakra energy into your home: it is all about creating a welcoming space to greet all those who come into it.

Go outside now, and come back into your home. What is the first impression that you receive? Is it piles of clutter and a hallway full of stuff you leave there all the time? How does this appear to someone when they come in to your home? Often these thoughts only occur to people when they are thinking of selling a house, but you live there all the time, and perhaps it's time to look at this now?

Cherishing your guests

Sacral Chakra energy is all about sharing, being open, being with other people and making them feel welcome. In many cultures the idea of showing hospitality to a guest is sacred; they have the honoured place by the fireside, the best seat at the table. By showing this kind of generosity, the owner of the home receives positive energy from the guest in return.

Thinking about your space, where are the places where you and your family or friends gather? It might be sitting around a kitchen or dining room table, or on sofas and chairs in a lounge. Have a look at those spaces and ask yourself, 'How could I make these more welcoming?' It might mean buying some new cushions or a throw or two to make a sofa look more inviting. Rearranging furniture can make a space feel more open. Fresh flowers add touches of nature, and your windows might benefit from a good clean to let in sparkling light.

Warming colours

In the kitchen, Sacral Chakra tones like apricot or soft shades of orange or terracotta on walls can create a welcoming feel; colourful tablecloths and curtains can transform more neutral colours and surfaces. Play with Sacral Chakra energy in your welcoming spaces and watch your friends and family react to the changes.

Solar Plexus Chakra: Home as an Energizing Space

The Solar Plexus Chakra is symbolized by the sun with its light, power and energy. Maximizing Solar Plexus Chakra energy in your home means finding the place where the most daylight comes in and making that place even more open.

Walk around your rooms and think about this. Perhaps you have never noticed where the most light is; or how the light changes during the day as the sun moves across the sky.

Windows are the obvious way to let light into a room; keeping them clean and sparkling inside and out lets in brightness and keeps the energy of the inside space refreshed. Opening windows when the weather permits to let fresh air and light into your space is even better.

Reflecting light

In the Chinese art of feng shui, the placement of certain objects is important to keep energy flowing and moving in a space, avoiding stagnation. Mirrors on walls are key here: they reflect the light and brighten rooms, even where the sun does not shine in. Hanging large mirrors in small rooms can totally transform the space.

Light can also be reflected through natural crystals such as clear quartz, citrine (golden quartz) or cut glass hanging crystals that refract light into wonderful rainbow hues. Using these light-filled objects adds a final energizing touch to a room.

Listen to your instincts

Solar Plexus Chakra energy is an important expression of personal energy and power. Choosing crystals that you feel instinctively drawn to and placing them where your intuition guides you is a very positive way to enhance your Solar Plexus energy in your home. Larger crystals can be a strong point of focus in a room; you may find you move them a few times before you find exactly the right spot to place them. By doing this you are intuitively enhancing your own personal energy in your space.

Heart Chakra: Home as a Green Space

Green is one of the main colours associated with the Heart Chakra. Being such a vital colour of nature, it makes sense that a wonderful way to enhance Heart Chakra energy in your space is to look at all the places where you can bring in the energy of plants and flowers.

If you have a garden attached to your home, this is the obvious place to start. The more you interact with your garden and the plants in it, the more you are enhancing your own Heart Chakra energy. How does your garden space work for you? If it feels like more of a nuisance than a pleasure, then consider how you could enhance it so it is more inviting to be in. Getting professional help can transform a dull conventional lawn and flower beds, breaking up space with curving lines or creating new places for plants; if your garden slopes, adding terraces can make interesting zones to plant at different levels. If you find it hard to bend down to do weeding, think about putting in raised beds so that you can get at the plants more easily. Having a garden is such a blessing; the more time you spend in it, the more your Heart Chakra energy is enhanced.

Using limited space

Living in a flat might give you a balcony, an ideal space for a container garden with pots; you can grow flowers, or vegetables like baby tomatoes or mini courgettes, or herbs to add flavours to your cooking. If you live in a flat with no balcony, you can still bring green energy inside your home in the form of house plants and flowers. Spider plants help to neutralize negative energy in the house; a warm inner climate can favour beautiful exotic species like orchids. Placing plants in your space is a lovely intuitive way to feel where you would like green Heart Chakra energy to be.

Throat Chakra:
Home as an Expression of You

Making your own space is a very deep human instinct. The Throat Chakra gives us the energy to make these statements about personal identity, whether through the words we speak or the things we choose to have around us to reflect who we are.

Have you ever noticed how personalizing space is so important to people? For example, on a train, once passengers get on, in very little time the place where each person sits becomes unique to them, with their own arrangement of personal belongings, coats, scarves and gadgets; if a family is occupying seats, a whole area very quickly becomes their own! Or on a beach, as holidaymakers arrive, watch how quickly each person stakes a claim on a space by arranging their belongings around a towel. Arranging a comfortable place around us is something we all do.

Taking this further into the space where you live, what you see around you, the way you arrange things and the way the space feels are all expressions of you. Look around your home now and try to take it in as if you were seeing it for the first time. How well do you think it reflects you? How would you like it to reflect you more?

Self-expression at home

Exercising personal creativity to make a space your own is exciting, freeing and empowering. The pictures you put on walls, the books on shelves, the cushions on the sofa, the rugs on the floor, even the colours of the walls: everything around you is there by your choice. If you want to bring more Throat Chakra energy into your space, ask yourself as you look around: what do you feel reflects you, or what does not serve you any more? Be brave and let go of things that are of the past. Let the energy of the Throat Chakra guide you to create a space that really 'sings' of you.

Third Eye Chakra: Home as a Creative Space

If you have been working on your Third Eye Chakra lately, you may be finding that you are inspired to be more creative in your life. Making a special space in your home to practise your creativity can enhance this process even more.

If we revisit the idea of the 'den' from childhood, it was a special space, full of the colours and things that helped us visit our own creative world. It might have been a tree house, where as children we went to get away from grown-ups, or a garage or an attic where we were allowed to hang out with our friends.

The dens of adulthood can be varied. Something as simple as a garden shed can be transformed into something truly unusual and individual. If you are interested in green and sustainable buildings, have a look at eco-pods that can be installed in an outside space. Inside the home, there might be a room that is underused or a bedroom that is no longer occupied that can be transformed into a creative haven. If all your space is occupied or you share it with other people, you can still find a way to create an inspirational place; for example, in a room that is your own, you can decide to set aside part of it using a decorated screen to make a particular area feel special.

Make it happen in your space

The idea of the den is that it is a special space, one where your very own creative energy takes form in the ways that excite and interest you. Painting, playing music, photography, sewing, writing: whatever your passion is, you can set it up and leave it in this space to come back to whenever you want. It's a space to work with the Third Eye Chakra, a place to create your own kind of magic and use the inspiration from your energy work.

Crown Chakra: Home as a Sacred Space

In many countries, particularly in the Far East, ordinary homes have small shrines or altars inside, decorated with fresh flowers each day and scented by burning incense. This is a tradition going back centuries: the ancestors of a family are honoured in the family shrine, or a particular spiritual teacher like the Buddha is honoured with a statue in a special place. This practice creates sacred space inside the home; focusing on this space links to the Crown Chakra and the expression of spiritual energy.

Setting up an altar in your home is a wonderful way to bring spiritual energy into your space. You may choose to place religious symbols on it, but this is not necessary: it can just be a place where you put any objects that have spiritual meaning to you.

Placing your shrine

Thinking about where to place your altar is important; it could be that you have already found a favourite place to do your meditations and yoga as part of your chakra energy practice. Creating an altar here would help to focus the energy of your chakra work.

A small, low table is ideal to work with; place a cloth over it in a colour that you like, or perhaps a multi-coloured cloth or scarf if you prefer. A vase for fresh flowers, a base for a candle or nightlight, and an incense holder are important items; the flowers bring the energy of nature to your altar and the candle and incense purify your space. Then you may choose to add other elements that are meaningful to you: crystals, beach stones, small statues, feathers, all placed as you wish. Daily lighting a candle and incense and keeping the flowers fresh is the act of tending your altar, bringing the beautiful spiritual energy of the Crown Chakra into your space.

The Chakra Journey: Starting Simply

As we have seen on the journey through this book, the exploration of the chakras is a fascinating way to add spiritual meaning to life. From looking at the chakras individually and practising ways to energize them, to recognizing signs of chakra energy in daily life and developing that energy in your work and personal space, this practice is life-enhancing and expands personal awareness.

Having reached this point, you may be wondering where to begin. The important thing is to do just that: to set your feet on the path.

The joy of learning

One suggestion is to go back to Chapter 2 on the individual chakras and start to get to know them by following the suggested exercises. Some chakra energies will already feel familiar; that is a sign that they are working well. Others may feel more of a challenge, meaning that practising the energy exercises will energize and strengthen those levels.

This is a journey of discovery, so go slowly, feel your way, sense what works for you, and be gentle with yourself. The journey is meant to be fun, inspirational, magical and expansive; the more steps you take, the more you will want to explore. Approach the journey with a sense of curiosity and kindness to yourself.

Most of all: enjoy it!

"A journey of a thousand miles
begins with one step."
LAO TZU

GLOSSARY

SANSKRIT TERMS

Asana a posture in yoga.

Ayurveda the ancient Indian 'science of life', incorporating spirituality, medicine, yoga, diet and health.

Bija literally translates as 'seed sound'; ancient individual sounds for the chakras.

Chakra meaning 'wheel'; the word to describe the energy centres of the human system.

Mantra a series of sacred Sanskrit words making a phrase that is chanted, e.g Om mani padme hum.

Prana the life energy of the human body, transmitted from the cosmic source into the human form and passed along the spine through the chakras.

OTHER TERMS

Aromatherapy the use of essential oils to help with mental, physical and emotional well-being.

Aromatherapy fragrance burner or vaporizer a flame-driven or electrical unit used to warm essential oils and spread the aroma into a space.

Aura a field of energy that permeates and surrounds the human body. Some people with sensitive healing abilities can see it as a field of colours around a person. The chakra colours show up in the aura as stronger or weaker shades depending on how well they are functioning.

Breastbone a strong bony area in the centre of the chest which holds the two sides of the rib cage together. It is the physical location of the Heart Chakra.

Colour vibration the seven colours of the rainbow (also the seven main chakra colours) are the main colours that we see. All colours are vibrations of light; white light has the fastest vibration, black the slowest, and all the chakra colours in between vary in intensity. For example, the violet of the Crown Chakra is a much higher vibration than the slower, denser vibration of the red Root Chakra.

Dowsing ancient energy sensing practice using a pendulum, a weight on a string, to give yes and no answers.

Endocrine system the hormone system of the entire body. The human body produces many different hormones, for example to influence sleep, mood or menstruation in women.

Energy in healing, the term is used to describe a force that permeates all the universe and all living things. In Chinese medicine it is called *chi* and in Indian Ayurvedic practice it is called *prana*.

Essential oil a pure natural aroma extracted from a single plant, fruit, herb, wood or flower.

Feng Shui an ancient Chinese art which balances the flow of energy through a space, such as a home, by using particular objects placed in special locations.

Healing the art of bringing energy into balance within a person, using many different tools, such as colour, sound, essential oils/aromatherapy or massage.

Holistic healing the bringing about of a balance of mind, body and spirit by any of the means of healing.

Hormone a regulatory substance produced by the body to influence specific organs, tissues or systems.

Incense natural aromatic resins and herbs ground into paste to coat incense sticks, or sold as loose powder to burn on charcoal.

Meditation a practice of stilling and calming the mind, sitting in a relaxed but focused posture, using breathing exercises or visualizations to reach a state of inner peace.

Sacrum a large bony area in the shape of a triangle, at the base of the spine.

Self-healing a healing practice that you apply to yourself. It is a calming and soothing activity which promotes relaxation and peace.

Sixth sense in healing, the five regular senses – sight, hearing, smell, taste and touch – are said to be enhanced by the sixth sense, intuition – a flash of sudden inspired knowing.

FURTHER READING

ON CHAKRAS

Osho *The Chakra Book: Energy and Healing Power of the Subtle Body* (Osho Foundation, 2015)

Liz Simpson *The Book of Chakra Healing* (Gaia Classics, 2017)

Doreen Virtue *Chakra Healing: Awakening Your Spiritual Power to Know and Heal* (Hay House, 2004)

Ambika Wauters *The Book of Chakras* (Barrons Educational Series, 2002)

ON YOGA

Tara Fraser *Yoga for You: A Step by Step Guide to Yoga at Home for Everybody* (Watkins, 2008)

BKS Iyengar *Yoga: The Path to Holistic Health* (DK, 2014)

Charice Kiernan *The Yoga Bible for Beginners* (Author, 2017)

Kassandra Reinhardt *Yin Yoga: Stretch the Mindful Way* (DK, 2018)

Sivananda Yoga Vedanta Centre *Yoga: Your Home Practice Companion* (DK, 2010)

ON AROMATHERAPY

Susan Curtis *Neal's Yard Remedies: Essential Oils* (DK, 2016)

Patricia Davis *Aromatherapy: An A–Z* (Ebury, 2011)

Jennie Harding *The Essential Guide to Oils* (Watkins, 2008)

Jennie Harding *Aromatherapy Massage for You* (Duncan Baird Publishers, 2005)

Julia Lawless *The Encyclopedia of Essential Oils* (Thorsons, 2012)

ON COLOUR HEALING

Theo Gimbel *The Colour Therapy Workbook* (Thorsons, 2002)

June McLeod *Colours of the Soul: Transform Your Life Through Colour Therapy* (O Books, 2006)

Howard Sun and Dorothy Sun *Colour Your Life: How to Use the Right Colours to Achieve Balance, Health and Happiness* (Piatkus, 2012)

Pauline Wills *The Colour Healing Manual* (Singing Dragon, 2003)

ON SOUND HEALING

Jonathan Goldman *The Humming Effect: Sound Healing for Health and Happiness* (Healing Arts Press, 2017)

ON CRYSTAL HEALING

Lucy Gemson *Crystals: The Complete Beginner's Guide* (Author, 2016)

Judy Hall *The Crystal Bible Vols 1, 2, 3* (Godsfield Press, 2009, 2009, 2013)

Judy Hall *The Little Book of Crystals* (Gaia, 2016)

Jennie Harding *Secrets of Crystals* (Ivy Press, 2007)

USEFUL WEBSITES

CHAKRA HEALING
Mindbodygreen
www.mindbodygreen.com

Chakra Healing
www.chakrahealing.com

YOGA
British Wheel of Yoga
www.bwy.org.uk

Iyengar Yoga
www.iyengaryoga.org.uk

Sivananda Yoga Centre
www.sivananda.org/london

AROMATHERAPY
Tisserand Aromatherapy
www.tisserand.com

Quinessence Aromatherapy
www.quinessence.com

Oshadhi Essential oils
www.oshadhi.co.uk

National Association for
Holistic Aromatherapy
www.naha.org

Alliance of International
Aromatherapists
www.alliance-aromatherapists.org

International Aromatherapy and
Aromatic Medicine Association
www.iaama.org.au

SOUND HEALING
The College of Sound Healing
www.collegeofsoundhealing.co.uk

British Academy of Sound Therapy
www.britishacademyofsoundtherapy.com

Sound Healers Association
www.soundhealersassociation.org

Vibrational Sound Association
www.vibrationalsoundassociation.com

Australian Holistic Healers' Association
www.ahhca.org

CRYSTAL HEALING
British Academy of Crystal Healing
www.britishacademyofcrystalhealing.co.uk

Association of Melody Crystal Healing
Instructors
www.taomchi.com

Australian Crystal Healing Centre
www.crystalsoundandlight.com

INDEX

ACKNOWLEDGEMENTS

AUTHOR ACKNOWLEDGEMENTS

I would like to thank everyone at Ivy Press for their attention to detail in the production of this book. I also thank some of my most important mentors and influencers in my healing career, namely Greta Gill and Andrew Ferguson on chakras and their energies, Robert Tisserand on aromatherapy, Richard Scull on crystals, Paddy Baillie on sound healing and Belinda Thompson on yoga.

This book is dedicated to all my healing friends – near and far.

PICTURE ACKNOWLEDGEMENTS

The publisher would like to thank the following for permission to reproduce copyright material:

Alamy Stock Photo/Image Source: 40 (left); Johner Images: 203; Mariusz Szczawinski: 83; Radius Images: 211; Westend61 GmbH: 167. **Ivy Press/**John Woodcock: 19. **Prashanthns/**CC BY-SA 3.0: 13. **Shutterstock/**Africa Studio: 145, 147 (far right); Alex Segre: 177; Alexander Raths: 40 (right); AmyLv: 146 (centre left); Atosan: 179; Berislav Kovacevic: 205; Brandon Heiss: 173; Christian Bertrand: 64 (left); Cultura Motion: 71; Denis Belitsky: 213; DGLimages: 28; Fabrizio Misson: 187; Feyyaz Alacam: 59; fizkes: 9; Flexey: 53 (left); Gamzova Olga: 146 (centre right); haveseen: 195; iko: 183; ImageFlow: 113; Jacob Lund: 181, 201; Julia Metkalova: 165; Karelian: 47; Kazmulka: 147; KucherAV: 41 (top); Kzenon: 64 (right); lightpoet: 127; Luna Vandoorne: 35; MediaGroup_BestForYou: 166; Microgen: 172, 175; Monkey Business Images: 189, 191, 207, 209; Narong Jongsiriku: 164; Nikodash: 77; Ocskay Mark: 14; Olga Zelenkova: 4; Photographee.eu: 95, 193; Pixeljoy: 18; plprod: 144; PlusONE: 52; Roman Kosolapov: 185; S.Borisov: 65; S.SITTA H: 146 (far left); shooarts: 53 (right); Sollex: 19; Swapan Photography: 147; Syda Productions: 197; Symonenko Viktoriia: 41 (bottom); Tatyana Chaiko: 76; TijanaM: 2; Trybex: 173; vasanty: 23 (top); wavebreakmedia: 107, 117; ZephyrMedia: 112.

All reasonable efforts have been made to trace copyright holders and to obtain their permission for the use of copyright material. The publisher apologizes for any errors or omissions in the list above and will gratefully incorporate any corrections in future reprints if notified.